GW00818787

ONE MORE STEP

The Reverend Margaret Cundiff was born in Somerset but has lived in the north of England since early childhood. Since 1973 she has served on the staff of St James' Church, Selby, in North Yorkshire, and was ordained deacon in 1987 and priest in 1994. She is also Broadcasting Officer for the diocese of York and broadcasts frequently both locally and nationally. She has contributed regularly to BBC Radio 2's *Pause for Thought*, and to the British Forces Broadcasting Service's religious programmes.

Also by Margaret Cundiff

Called to be Me and *Following On* (Bumper Edition)
I'd Like You to Meet . . .
My Kind of Day
Travelling Light – through Mark's Gospel

MARGARET CUNDIFF

ONE MORE STEP

For Maureen,

Every blessing

Margaret Cundiff

TRI△NGLE

First published 1995
Triangle
SPCK
Holy Trinity Church
Marylebone Rd
London NW1 4DU

Copyright © Margaret Cundiff 1995

All rights reserved. No part of this book may be reproduced or
transmitted in any form or by any means, electronic or
mechanical, including photocopying, recording, or by any
information storage and retrieval system, without permission in
writing from the publisher.

ACKNOWLEDGEMENTS

Bible quotations are from the Revised Standard Version of the
Bible © 1946, 1952, 1971 by the Division of Christian Education
of the National Council of Churches of Christ in the USA.

The hymn 'Tell out, my soul' (p. 78) is copyright
Timothy Dudley-Smith (b. 1926).

The song 'Will you come and follow me' (p. 109) is by
John L. Bell and Graham Maule. From *Heaven Shall Not Wait*
(Wild Goose Songs Vol. 1); copyright The Iona Community,
Pearce Institute, 840 Govan Road, Glasgow G51 3UU.

The song 'One More Step' (pp. xi, 126) by Sydney Carter is from
Songs of Sydney Carter – Book 4. Reproduced by permission of
Stainer & Bell Ltd.

British Library Cataloguing-in-Publication Data
A catalogue record for this book is available from the
British Library

ISBN 0-281-04796-0

Typeset by Dorwyn Ltd, Rowlands Castle, Hants
Printed and bound in Great Britain by BPC Paperbacks Ltd
Member of the British Printing Company Ltd

For my husband Peter

Acknowledgements

My grateful thanks to those who first set my feet on the right path in life and on my journey of faith; those who have walked with me, prayed for me and encouraged me through the years, and those who are my travelling companions today. My family, Peter, Julian and Alison, who so cheerfully support me by their love and understanding, and the family of the Church, both in Selby and in the York Diocese, particularly as I came to be ordained priest in York Minster on the Eve of Pentecost, 1994. Fran and Ian who translated my typing into a beautifully presented manuscript, and Geoff Green for an excellent cover photograph. Special thanks to all at SPCK and to Rachel Boulding, my editor, and Myrtle Powley for their professional wisdom and personal friendship. And last, but not least, to the staff and children of Wistow School, past and present, who have so cheerfully sung along with me 'our' theme song, 'One More Step', at our Friday morning school assemblies through the years.

MARGARET CUNDIFF

Contents

Contents

Preface

Among all the other files in my office cabinet is one marked 'Women Priests'. It is a bulky file, dating back over a number of years. It contains press cuttings and reports, articles, Synod documents, letters. There are notes of press conferences, facts and figures, and conference material – all the pros and cons surrounding the long debate on the issue of women priests. As a broadcasting officer, part of my work is to keep the media informed about Church issues, and also to help the Church deal with the media, not just on this particular matter but on all aspects of the life and work of the Church. As I see it, my job is to help bridge the gap between the media and the Church, getting them to understand one another, to co-operate, and to respect each other's stance. I also try to encourage people in the Churches to make their voices heard, by writing, broadcasting, taking part in television programmes. For over ten years I was the Anglican Adviser to Yorkshire Television, and I still serve on a number of councils and committees concerned with the world of communications.

I try to present material fairly, giving access to all points of view, and putting forward names and situations which will help project the full story. This is not always easy when a subject is something

I feel strongly about, one way or the other, but I have honestly, and I hope successfully, tried to be disciplined enough to do so.

As a Broadcasting Officer for York diocese I am concerned with the whole range of thought and action, and it is a job I enjoy to the full, not least because I meet such interesting people, both in the media and the Church. I am also a broadcaster and writer in my own right, as Margaret Cundiff, sharing my life and my Christian belief with others. Among my greatest pleasures is being a regular contributor to *Pause for Thought* and other such radio programmes, and also writing a weekly column in my local paper, the *Selby Times*, as well as magazine articles in various periodicals and papers.

In my file marked 'Women Priests' are also personal reflections written down as the debate made its long and often wearisome progress. These were private comments, not to be used in press releases but to record for myself what I was doing and how I was feeling, to help me personally to understand what was going on within my life and ministry at the time. They helped me to get into perspective how these things affected the way I saw my future, and whatever the outcome, to be able to commit it all to God and accept whatever happened with grace, humour and faith.

Fourteen years ago I was asked by Triangle Books to write a book for them, telling the story of my life up to that point. It took some time for me to agree. Who, I argued, would be interested in the story of a north of England deaconess who also worked in the communications business? More to the point, would I dare to chronicle the ups and downs of my life? It was the then Bishop of Selby, Morris Maddocks, who decided the issue for me.

Bishop Morris asked me a question: 'Are you ashamed of what God has done in your life?'

When I answered 'No', he replied, 'Go and write the book.'

The book was entitled *Called To Be Me*, and was the forerunner of several others.

Today, in late 1994, I am still in Selby, ministering in the same parishes. The big difference is that I am now a priest, one of the first women to be ordained priest in the Church of England in this country. I am still a broadcasting officer, involved in the media alongside my parochial work. This book is a continuation of *Called To Be Me*, and I have found it most useful to go back through my file marked 'Women Priests', with my personal reflections along the way. This is my story, of the way God has led me, what has happened to me, the people and situations which have been so much part of my journey, and how it is for me now. Yet this book is already history, for even as I write now and you read what I have written, life has gone on, and who knows what may have changed?

One of my favourite songs which we sing regularly at the village school assembly is:

One more step along the world I go,
One more step along the world I go.
From the old things to the new,
Keep me travelling along with you.
And it's from the old I travel to the new,
Keep me travelling along with you.

This is my prayer each day, that whatever happens I will keep travelling with my Lord, the one who called me to follow him many years ago, who still calls me to serve him, calls and enables me 'to be me', the real Margaret Cundiff!

So come and join me as I step out, share my journey. And may the Lord bless and encourage you in your journey, too, as you take 'one more step' along your way today.

1

The Motion is Carried

The two pieces of paper sat neatly together on my desk, like Siamese twins. Alike in size, shape and format. On each, four short paragraphs, the same length, the same style, written by the same person. Each identically dated, each signed at the bottom boldly and firmly, like a formal document or business letter. In fact, you could say, very businesslike. They were so alike you could be forgiven for thinking they were duplicates, unless you had picked them up and read them. Then you would have discovered that their contents were completely opposite. The same day, the same writer, and addressed to the same people – and yet so different. The clue lay in the date; they were both written during the morning of Wednesday, November 11th, 1992, the day the General Synod was to vote on the ordination of women to the priesthood. I knew that, following the vote, the press would be on to me for my reaction – two newspapers had already made arrangements to ring me as soon as the result of the vote was announced – and I wanted to be ready, whichever way it went. So I had sat down, prayed hard that I would be given the right words, and then prepared two statements, one which began, 'I am, of course, saddened by the decision . . .', the other, 'Of course, I am overjoyed . . .'.

So there they were, prepared and ready; but which piece of paper would I be picking up later that afternoon? I would just be glad when it was all over, whichever way it went. I was tired of hearing all the old arguments trotted out on both sides, tired of the way the whole thing had been used to create animosity and division, much of which had not existed prior to the constant party manoeuvring, stirring up and exploitation of the subject by the media and interested bodies for stories.

Wearing my 'communications hat' I had tried to help to prepare other people to cope with the result of the vote, had urged calm and restraint in the expression of sorrow or joy, and had even, with colleagues working in the media, organised a training day for women deacons to help them cope with the inevitable media interest. That day, held several months previously, had been a fascinating experience. To be sure, it had only been a dummy run, quite different from the atmosphere there would be on the actual day of the vote, but it was the graceful yet firm way in which they all responded to questioning which made me realise afresh the strength of character, conviction and depth of spirituality of my fellow deacons. As they were faced that day with their own response to a possible yes or no, what came over was their calm, unswerving and loyal commitment to the service of God and of other people.

As November 11th drew nearer I began to realise how much warmth and support there was for me, not just from family, friends and church members, but from people who were known to me only by sight. Those I saw in the local shops or the market, with whom I normally exchanged a smile or greeting, now went out of their way to talk to me – one lady almost got run over dashing across the road in the rain because, she said, 'I wanted just to have a word and say good luck.' But I think it was the shyly shared memories that touched me most. Because they knew the issue meant so much to me, people overcame their natural reserve and told me their own stories, recalling occasions when I had taken a friend's baby's baptism, or a family funeral, or when something I had written in my column in the local paper or said on radio had particularly helped them. They had not forgotten, and they just wanted to say thank you. Many of those encounters in the street began with the words, 'I don't suppose you will remember it, love, but . . . and I'd like to wish you all the best . . .' Sometimes the support was quite physical – like the time I was gazing into the frozen food cabinet in the local supermarket, trying to decide between peas and beans, when I was thumped so hard on the back by a burly young man that I nearly joined the packs of.vegetables head on. 'Best of luck for next week, mate, hope it goes OK for you,' he muttered, and then he was off with his trolley load like a rally driver approaching the final bend. Then, of course, there were those who carefully saved for me all the newspaper cuttings to do with the ordination of women, or began conversations with 'Did you see on telly last night that vicar who said . . .?'

So when the day finally did dawn, there was a certain sense of relief that, come what may, afterwards there would be other subjects of conversation. Until then there was a certain sense of being in limbo, and I was anxious to be able to concentrate on other things, without having that feeling of the unknown, of wondering not just how I would feel but how I would react. The Bishop of Selby, Humphrey Taylor, had kindly invited all the women deacons in his area to 'open house' at his home in York on the day of the vote, with the opportunity just to pop in for tea, coffee or hot soup, to watch the television coverage, to be together on the day, and to share whatever the outcome might be. As he said, 'None of us knows what is going to happen, or how we shall feel – let's be together . . .' His invitation and concern meant so much to all of us; he really was a 'father in God' to us, a proper dad!

The Bishop's house, situated behind York Minster, is a square and solid-looking building, with an air of formality befitting its position in Precentor's Court, among the other elegant houses which grace the immediate surroundings of the Minster. You could say there are shades of Barchester, as in many English cathedral closes: formal on the outside, but inside an air of warm informality. Coming in from the cold on that November morning I was struck by the relaxed atmosphere. Fortified by coffee and conversation, I soon forgot the worries and anxieties that had been building up over the last few days. It was, I am sure, due to the fact that we were together, women who had been in ministry in many different areas, but with the same deep hope that one day the Church might decide the time was right to ordain women as priests. It was this togetherness that released the tension and strain. We were not on our own, but in it together, and we would continue to be together, whatever happened. Somehow that was more important, even more real than what was happening in London, and I was glad of that!

Coffee, soup, warmth, conversation and the constant comings and goings made the time fly by, but it was as we settled down to watch the debate that some of the feelings of foreboding returned to me. What of the future? I was loath to leave the safety and security of that gathering, but knew I must be home before the debate ended, ready for the press. I drove back with my ears glued to the radio, following the debate all the way. Arriving home, I busied myself with all the practical things, like preparing tea. My husband, Peter, who I knew felt equally concerned about the vote, was keeping a low profile. He was there and available, but not in any way commenting or asking questions; he knew there would be time enough for that afterwards. Then came the wait for the announcement of the result. I sat bolt upright in front of the television set: it seemed a very long time in coming, and the Archbishop of Canterbury looked very solemn and severe.

It has been said that before death your life flashes before you; mine certainly did in those moments before the result of the vote was announced. I knew it would be close, and I feared it would be a 'no', but then I told myself firmly, 'You have been a deacon now for over five years, something you had never really expected. You have been allowed such enormous privileges in the ministry of the Church, and look what you have come through, with all the mistakes as well! Life has been a bonus, be grateful and thankful.'

In my life I had seen the role of women in ministry expand tremendously, opening up opportunities and responsibilities beyond our wildest hopes and dreams. I thought of my own ministry in Selby over

5

the previous twenty years, since I was licensed as a lay worker, then as a deaconess and finally ordained deacon. The Church had moved forward so much, even in the last five years. I was blessed indeed to be part of the Church in these times and, whatever happened, I had a very fulfilling ministry both in the parish and in my media work. Anyway, at the age of sixty . . .

At two minutes past five the Archbishop gave the results. Never good at working out percentages, my mind could hardly take in the significance of the figures. Then came the historic announcement, 'The motion is carried.' I sat still, my eyes fixed on the television set, and in a very matter-of-fact voice said to my husband, 'Oh, it's gone through, that's good', and promptly burst into tears. Peter rushed across and put his arms round me. 'Don't cry, it's gone through, it's all right. I'm so pleased . . .' I am sure in many homes at that moment a similar scene was being re-enacted!

That evening passed like a dream, with people endlessly coming and going. The first arrival was the local Methodist minister who had been visiting someone up the road from us. Hearing the result, she had run down the road and was through our front door in moments. Her visit was of special significance as we already worked together in the village, and she, being a woman minister, knew how I felt – after all, she had gone through it herself. So Julia's arrival somehow set a very special note of celebration. Then my vicar arrived with flowers. He pushed them into my arms very self-consciously, saying, 'These were all I could get . . .', and then crushed me and the flowers in his embrace. I was able to detach myself sufficiently to put on my 'communications hat' and deal with the press. I read out – with great joy – one of my prepared statements, the one which began 'Of course, I am overjoyed . . .'

Amid all the celebrations our son Julian arrived home from work. Seeing the crowd in the sitting room he fled upstairs, with the briefest of greetings to us all, only to emerge quickly to collect his tea. Our daughter Alison had been on the telephone from London as soon as the vote was announced, full of congratulations and jokes, telling me of what was happening all around her, and sending congratulations from her friends. She was nearer to it all than I was, for she works for the Church Commissioners and, being in Westminster, had seen all the comings and goings that day. She was bubbling over with excitement, and so I was a little disappointed that Julian had not been equally enthusiastic. But then I had forgotten that, though they are brother and sister, they are very different characters. I was reminded of that on the following day when Julian arrived home, this time to a quieter atmosphere. He came in with flowers and a card: 'These are for you, mum. I didn't want to give them to you last night when all those people were here. I am ever so pleased. Congratulations!' Yes, people have their own way of sharing their feelings. I was to find that out in the days and weeks that followed.

For the moment, I heaved a sigh of relief, offered up a prayer of thanksgiving, and got on with what needed doing there and then. After all, life goes on, whatever happens: 'the daily round, the common task'. Tomorrow was another day, today was here, and for the moment, it contained sufficient to keep me well and truly occupied!

2
Sixty – Not Out!

After the initial excitement, relief and great thanksgiving, came the inevitable low. The ominous rumbles that predicted a stormy time ahead rose to shrill crescendos from the opponents of women priests. It was clear that every possibility of overturning the decision would be explored, and there were some very confident claims that, although the decision had been made by the Church to ordain women as priests, it could still be a long time before it actually happened. Dates were suggested, and then promptly disputed, but it finally looked as though, 'all being well', the first ordinations would take place in the spring or summer of 1994.

I soon decided that, whatever happened, it was no use getting all steamed up about what might or what might not happen in the future. November was rapidly turning into December and all the Christmas arrangements loomed large. As I juggled with Christmas shopping, scripts for Christmas broadcasts and parish activities, thoughts about 'when, how and if' took a back seat in my mind. Frankly, I had not got the time to be thinking about it, and besides I was becoming more than a little confused as to what really was happening. 'First things first' – and there were enough contenders for first place in that run-up to Christmas, not least getting my Christmas letters off. Each year I write a 'round robin' of family news, adding personal bits at the end for individual friends. I began this many years ago when I realised I was writing the same sort of letter to most people at Christmas, and there were so many to write it was akin to writing lines at school. So I hit on the printed letter, not a new idea judging by the many we receive each year. Two paragraphs I had written were particularly significant in that letter for Christmas 1992:

> The great news this year for Margaret has been the vote in favour of women priests, and so hopefully she will be offering when the time comes. In the meantime she is kept as busy as usual . . .

> During the year both Peter and Margaret celebrated their sixtieth birthdays, and Margaret is rejoicing in all the concessions old age brings, especially having a rail card much used – while continuing to enjoy life as the eternal teenager . . .

It was as I sat looking at what I had written that the realisation of my age in relation to the possibility of being ordained priest hit me. In the space of several seconds I suffered panic, despair, hope, and more panic again. There it was, in black and white, 'sixtieth birthday'. And although I had cheerfully put 'continuing to enjoy life as the eternal teenager', I knew that what counted was my birth certificate and not my attitude to the years. If it was, as had been estimated, that the earliest a woman could be ordained priest was 1994, even if I camped out on the Archbishop's doorstep – which was not a good plan – or if the diocese of York decided to be one of the first dioceses to ordain, as they had been when we were ordained deacons, I could not escape the fact I would by then be sixty-two. Now I have never worried about age and the passing years, treating every birthday as an occasion for celebration, but not everyone saw it like that. Maybe I had passed my 'sell-by date', and although women would be ordained priests in 1994 or whenever, it would be too late for me. That was it! I needed time to think this one out, and so I looked in my diary, saw a free morning, put a line through it and said firmly to myself, 'Now is the time to think this through honestly before God, to be willing to accept whatever happens with his good grace.'

So later that week I set off down to the church, 'I'll be back around lunch time,' I told Peter, 'I've got a few things to do, a couple of calls to make.' I drove into the town, which was looking cheerfully festive with the Christmas tree in the market place and lights and decorations strung across the main street, and already busy with the shoppers pouring into town. I did a quick dash around the super-market and, putting my bags away in the boot of my car, parked outside church, unlocked the door and made my way to the vestry, where I knew I would not be disturbed. Around the walls hung photographs of the former vicars, dating back to the 1860s, up to the present, and the last framed photograph of all was of me in cassock and surplice like all the rest, but with my deacon's stole rather than a black scarf. The inscription under the photograph read, 'Margaret Cundiff. Parish Worker 1973. Deaconess 1977. Parish Deacon 1987.'

The memories came flooding back. Nearly twenty years in this parish, yet the story had begun long before. How long? Hard to say, really! I thought about it. Nearly fifty years I suppose it had been, since those days when as a youngster I had looked at my vicar in Mossley, in Congleton, where I lived, and thought to myself, 'That's the sort of person I'd like to be.' It was not anything to do with priesthood, but it was all to do with godliness. I could not have explained it at the time, it was a shadowy, unformed feeling, but a recognition of God in a person's life, something, someone that made that man, the vicar, different.

The seed was sown, I am sure of that, and began to take root, and to grow through my teenage years until suddenly, or so it seemed, it popped up, responding to a speaker at a Youth for Christ rally in Hanley. The speaker, a Baptist minister called Alan Redpath, had faced the young people listening to him that night with the claims of Jesus Christ, and he finished by saying, 'You can either go God's way or your own way. You have to make your mind up. You have to decide.' That night I did decide to follow Jesus Christ, to put my life in his hands. It happened on the back of the bus, going home after the rally. I always remember that night, on the back of a Potteries Motor Traction bus. I had nothing to offer but enthusiasm, and youth, but it seemed enough.

By the time I was nineteen I was at theological college in Oxford, at twenty-one in a parish in Wolverhampton and by twenty-two had changed my mind! A spell in youth work, then into personnel management, wonderfully happy years working in the textile industry, meeting my husband, building a home together, having a family, a boy and a girl, what more did I need? Then in our late thirties we had come over the Pennines to Selby in North Yorkshire to make our home afresh, for Peter's work dictated we move – a move none of us relished; after all, we were settled in Cheshire, near our family and friends. Who wanted to up sticks and go to Yorkshire? Certainly not us, but you go where the work is.

And so to Yorkshire, and the unknown area of Selby, we had to go. Yet it was to prove all part of God's loving purpose for us, for a couple of years later God had got me by the scruff of my neck, and in no uncertain terms challenged me afresh with what I was doing with my life. In an ordinary morning service in the church where now I sat in the vestry as the Parish Deacon, God had reminded me of the decision I had made all those years ago on the back of that bus. He had said clearly, and audibly, 'Be filled with the Spirit,' – and I had said 'Yes' . . . and life had changed again. God, in his marvellous economy, had brought me to this place at a certain time, for a certain task. I had no need to look for it, it just happened. A local vicar was ill, I volunteered to 'help out'. Shortly afterwards my own vicar left, and it was decided that I should be licensed as an honorary parish worker. Later on I was accepted as a candidate for deaconess, and in 1987 was one of the first women to be ordained deacon in York Minster, still serving at St James', Selby, but by that time also fully engaged in radio and television work and, most surprising of all, in writing. My first book, published in 1982, told the story of my life so far, *Called To Be Me*. Its success, which came as a complete surprise, led to more books, and now here I was at the age of sixty wondering where the future lay for me now.

I looked up at the photograph of the smiling deacon, and at the last inscription under the photograph, 'Parish Deacon 1987'. God had been so good to me; not only had he called me to serve him all those years ago, he had even given me a second chance when I had failed so miserably the first time round. All I had to offer the first time was youth and enthusiasm; all I had to offer the second time was middle age and enthusiasm; what had I to offer now? I thought of my date of birth – and that rail card – and supposed it was now a case of old age and enthusiasm. What was it I so often said when people asked me how I had managed to do such a lot in my life? My usual reply was, 'God opens doors and I fall through them'. Yes, that was true. God had opened doors. All my life he had gone on opening doors, and when I fell over he picked me up, set me on my feet and set me straight again. All my life he had been doing that, knowing me as he did, with all my failures, impatience and selfishness. He still went on opening doors, allowing me to participate in the greatest adventure of life, sharing the good news of Jesus with others. Would he hold back now? Would the fact that I was sixty stop him working out his good purpose in my life? What did I really want?

I thought about that for a long time that morning: 'What do I really want, more than anything else?' In the silence that enfolded me, I knew the answer. All I wanted was to go on with God, wherever and whatever that was. He had never disappointed me, never let me down. I could look back over my life and see his hand at every stage, every twist and turn. I could trust him for the future, too. I walked down the church with a spring in my step, humming a tune – and then I remembered the words:

> How good is the God we adore!
> Our faithful, unchangeable friend:
> His love is as great as his power
> And knows neither measure nor end.

> 'Tis Jesus the first and the last;
> His Spirit will guide us safe home:
> We'll praise him for all that is past,
> And we'll trust him for all that's to come.

Then the sixty-year-old 'eternal teenager' locked the church door, and marched down the road to join the rest of the Christmas shoppers.

3

The Double Diamond

History was never my strong point at school. I really could not see the point of learning by heart lists of kings, queens, battles and events from the past. What concerned me was life here and now, not the 'dim and distant'. It took me many years to realise that to understand the present you need to know something of the past, to be able to trace where we have come from, the influences, happenings and thought patterns of past generations. It was not until my college days that I began to take an interest in early church history, to feel that those people were real people, and had something to say to me, if I would only take notice. Those church history lectures have had a lasting effect on my life and that of my family. Captivated by the life of the Emperor Julian, who lost his life in AD 363, I decided that if ever I married and had a son I would call him Julian. Our college principal, Miss Dorothy Barter-Snow, was horrified when I told her of my intention: 'You couldn't! – he was a pagan!' Pagan he might have been, but he had sparked off my interest in history, and as I told the principal very solemnly, 'It is a lovely name!' In 1963 our son was born, we called him Julian, and so far he is very happy to be Julian, although we took the precaution of giving him a second name should he ever feel unhappy to be bearing the same name as a failed emperor.

My interest in history has always been people-centred. Buildings leave me cold, museums and exhibitions fail to move me until a character comes to life in my mind. When that happens I am hooked and want to know more. This happened to me in my own church of St James', Selby. It is quite a modern church compared with others in the area, sitting as it does in the shadow of Selby Abbey, which goes back to Norman times. St James' was built in 1867, one of many in the industrial era up and down the country. Known as 'The Railwayman's Church' it was built for the railway workers and their families who lived in the little houses clustered around it, and was described rather snootily by an ecclesiastical historian as 'a Victorian pile of no architectural merit'. It was the founder who aroused my attention, a man named James Audus, born in 1781, who became 'Mr Selby' during the first half of the nineteenth century. A landowner, railway director, shipbuilder, banker, he had a finger in every pie in Selby and the surrounding area, in fact he owned most of the town. He was a generous man and, far ahead of his time, gave liberally of his time and talents, money and influence. In early life he had been taken to hear John Wesley preach and this had had a profound effect on him for life. Although a member of Selby Abbey he wanted a church in the town for the ordinary folk, where they could feel at home, and not have to pay a pew rent either – as was the custom then. So he built a district church on his land, as a thanksgiving to God for all the good things he had given him, not least the gift of faith, and also to provide for the people who wanted a homely church, a place where status mattered for nothing, only the desire to know and serve God. Over the years it has fulfilled its purpose, and still today is known for its friendly atmosphere, for having at its heart an evangelical thrust in its work and witness.

You could say all the clergy who have served at St James' have been of a certain type from the evangelical wing of the Church of England, and none more so than a great stalwart named the Reverend Samuel Froggatt, from Bradford, who was vicar in the 1920s. Under his ministry the church prospered, and even today stories about him abound. So here was another name to excite me, and make me want to know more. I began to delve into the records, discovering among other things that a great Diamond Jubilee was held in 1927. Finally I wrote down my findings and they were published, my first history book – how my history teacher would have been surprised! – the story of the church, from the life of James Audus, through the times of Samuel Froggatt to the present day.

It was as I was writing the book that the significance of two dates struck me. The church was built in 1867, and in 1927 had a great Diamond Jubilee celebration. We were fast approaching 1987 – the second Diamond Jubilee. I wondered, would a Double Diamond at St James' live up to that famous drink advert, 'A Double Diamond works wonders!'?

I suggested to the vicar that we should declare 1987 a year of celebration. He looked dubious, being used to my brainstorms. 'But Margaret, one hundred and twenty years isn't really special, why celebrate it?'

I had worked that one out. 'David, we both missed the centenary, and we are not likely to be here for the hundred and fiftieth! Why not celebrate our own Double Diamond?'

We decided to go ahead. The vision caught on. We celebrated all right, from a flower festival and youth events, to special services, concerts and an exhibition, even managing to trace the son of the famous Samuel Froggatt himself, a retired vicar from the West Country, Geoffrey Froggatt, who came to preach at the Harvest Festival.

Perhaps for me one of the greatest highlights of the year was a Victorian Weekend, when we had a Victorian social evening, all in costume of course, which included songs around the piano. I still remember the duet 'Have courage, my boy, to say no!' which two of us sang with tears in our eyes, trying not to explode into fits of giggles, to an audience doubled up with laughter at the sight of us in our Victorian costumes, bonnets and all. On the Sunday the vicar and I were again in costume, as were most of our congregation for services in nineteenth-century style, using the Book of Common Prayer. Looking out at our cheerful congregation I realised how many of them bore the same surnames as the ones I had discovered recorded in fading ink on yellowing pages in dusty records of the church. I recalled some words written by a clergyman of a neighbouring parish of that time: 'St James' Church, free and open, was at once filled with a motley but attached congregation of Wesleyans, Primitive Methodists, Congregationalists, nothingarians, and church folk . . .' I could almost see the look of disdain on his face when he penned those words. I could also see in my mind the people he had described, thronging into church in those far-off days, being made to feel welcome and at home. Maybe some of them were thought of as 'nothing-arians', for they had no background or education, no worldly possessions, but they soon realised how precious they were to God. 'Motley' – yes, they were varied characters all right, but prepared to pull to-gether, to be a family; and 'attached' – most cer-tainly. They discovered in this very ordinary little church, built for 'the working classes' the richness of the gospel, the treasures of the Bible, the joy of growing in their faith and experience and of bring-ing others into that same experience.

Today there are new names and faces as well, individuals and families who have come into the area from all over the country for work, for a new life, a new start. They have also been drawn into the church. Perhaps a neighbour or workmate has invited them along, the children have gone with friends to Sunday School or the youth group. Maybe something in the local paper has attracted them, or a poster, or just a sense of wanting to find out what was happening at that 'church around the corner' has brought them; and they have dis-covered, as those in the last one hundred and twenty years before them had discovered, that there was a welcome, an acceptance for them, a sense of coming home. 'Just like us,' I thought; we too had come as strangers, drawn in by love and prayer, warm hearts, open hands and a sense of faith and fun. So we had plenty to celebrate that 'Double Diamond' year.

It was a good time, being able to look back; but we could not stay in the past, as wistful nostalgia so easily fossilises. After all, look what happened to

Lot's wife – when she looked back, she turned into a pillar of salt. A church which continually looks back is in danger of becoming a lifeless monument to the past, lost in the passage of time.

The year 1987, though, was a very special one for me personally. On March 7th I was ordained as a deacon, by the Archbishop of York, in York Minster along with twenty-six other deaconesses serving in the York diocese. After all the years of discussion and debate the General Synod of the Church of England had finally said 'yes' to women deacons. What was the difference between a deaconess and a deacon? In many ways very little – after all the Order of Deaconesses had been in the Church of England for over a hundred years; but it was still a lay order, which meant that women were not regarded as being in 'holy orders' – part of the ordained ministry. The Archbishop of York, Dr John Habgood, writing about this to the diocese, said:

> On March 7th I shall be ordaining twenty-seven deaconesses to the Diaconate in the Minster. In one sense it is a small step – the tidying up of an anomaly which has nagged ever since the Order of Deaconesses was restored in the Church of England in 1861. Are they ordained or not? From March 7th onwards there will be no doubt. In another sense it is a very large step. Women will be clergy, with all that implies in terms of Synodical and legal status, and in the shared work of the Church at every level. In terms of worship the biggest change will be in the conduct of weddings . . . Please welcome our new Deacons, and pray for them and the parishes in which they

serve, that this acceptance of the role of women in the ordained ministry may bring blessings to all concerned.

So on March 7th I became the Reverend Margaret Cundiff, ordained into 'holy orders'. On that cold March day spring came early. There were signs of hope, just the smallest glimmer of hope, that one day, maybe even in my lifetime, women would be priests – but all that was a long time ahead, if ever. Margaret, the new deacon, full of the joys of spring, surrounded by family and friends, clutching a bunch of daffodils, looked with joy and renewed hope towards the future, the future of St James', with all those so-called 'nothingarians', the 'motley but attached' of which she was so proud to be a member. A new life was beginning, it would be strange at first, but it was going to be all right, she knew that. In a newspaper interview of that week I said:

It is a privilege and a responsibility because we are among the first women to be ordained. The eyes of the Church and the world will be upon us, so it is a bit awesome. A lot of the debate which follows will be about what people really think of us and our ministry. It could be the end of this century before women are actually allowed to become priests, I would love to be one of them, but I don't spend all my time thinking about it though.

As I read my own words I realise how much has happened in the last seven years, and what a privilege it has been to be a deacon at this particular time in the history of the Church. The seven years has been a labour of love, and has flown by, making it hard to believe it was so long. My prediction of women priests possibly by the end of the century was six years out, so there's a bonus of years!

Derek Jameson, with whom I worked for so long on BBC Radio Two with my *Pause for Thought* spots on his programme, called me his 'delightful deaconess'. I still think of those times on his programme as some of my favourite experiences. I never knew what he was going to come up with next. He was such a warm and wonderful character, and so supportive. I well remember on the show the week before I was ordained deacon, he was so excited and proud and announced, 'My Margaret's going to be a vicar!' I had to correct him on that one and try to explain what a deacon was. I loved being with him, for he had the gift of putting into words what most people would like to say or ask, but hadn't the nerve. Yet in doing so, he gave me the opportunity to say what I wanted to say about my faith and experiences, and to correct some of the myths that abound. I owe a great deal to Derek Jameson. He opened many doors of opportunity for me, and the night he interviewed me on *Wogan*, when he stood in for Terry Wogan, was one of the most frightening yet exciting nights of my life. God uses all sorts of people and situations to get the message across, I have found – even Derek Jameson and Margaret Cundiff on an early morning breakfast programme!

The programme, which went out live, meant going down to the London studio, or talking 'down the line' from Radio York, but one of the most memorable was when the whole of the morning show came from York Minster, which at that time was being restored after the fire which had done so much damage. Derek was fascinated and impressed by the magnificent Minster, and thoroughly enjoyed meeting many people engaged in the work in and around it. That morning I did my *Pause for Thought* standing beside the altar in the Minster, which for me – and I know for so many listeners – has a special significance. *Pause for Thought* has been nicknamed 'The God Slot' – it could not have come from a more appropriate location that Friday morning!

4
InterCity Encounter

I have never tried to work out how many miles I have travelled by rail over these last few years, but it must be many thousands. I was even a member of the Frequent Travellers Association until it was discontinued – but British Rail did give me two first-class tickets to travel anywhere in the country in one day to mark the closing down of the Association, so I did quite nicely! Peter and I went to Torquay for a day. Well, it did say ANYWHERE, and we worked out that the farthest we could go there and back in a day, and have a few hours to enjoy our destination, was Torquay, and so that's where we went. What a luxury it was travelling first class! We felt very grand, we had a most comfortable journey and the train was on time, too. When the guard came round for our tickets and we produced our 'specials', the couple across from us laughed and said 'Snap', as they too were travelling on the same offer. They were going even further than us, down to Cornwall, but had got on after us, so we reckon we both got about the same number of free miles.

It was a fun day, going first class, but that was a one-off; my journeys are normally far more ordinary. I serve on several committees and councils based in London and do a certain amount of broadcasting from London, so I know every bump in the rails,

every turn in the line on the InterCity from Doncaster to Kings Cross. I plan my journey like a mili-
tary exercise, getting the best possible deal
according to the times I need to travel, and of
course delighting in my Senior Rail Card – which
must have friction burns on it at times, it is so well
used. I allocate my travelling time to checking over
papers for the meetings I am going to, or refreshing
my mind with scripts or agendas. I give myself a
coffee break, time to read the paper and 'a bit of
peace and quiet', when I shut my eyes and allow the
rhythm of the journey to rock me, if not to sleep,
into a very contented and meditative frame of
mind. That is, of course, when my journey goes
according to my plan! Sometimes it goes quite the
opposite, and throws me out completely, but I have
often found that 'the God of surprises' has something in store for me which more than compensates
me for an enforced change in my routine.

I had such an experience one February morning.
It was typical winter weather, cold and dark, with
snow forecast. I had to catch an early train to London to make sure of being on time for my meeting
that morning. I had worked out that I had an hour
to get from Kings Cross to my meeting, just a couple
of tube stops, which would be more than enough,
and allowed for some delay on my journey. After all,
I could not expect trains to run exactly on time in
the depth of winter, and experience told me there
would probably be a few minutes added to my journey time. Peter drove me to Doncaster, the sky
darkening by the minute and the first ominous
flakes of snow falling, which by the time we got to
the station had become a blizzard. I was greatly
surprised, and delighted, when the train came in

right on time, and settled myself ready for the off. The train waited, and waited, and waited. There was a feeling of restlessness in the compartment, with much looking at watches and sighing. Then the announcement: 'This train is being delayed to await arrival of a train from York which will be terminating here.' A few minutes later came another announcement: 'This train is likely to be considerably delayed.' Now I am not the most patient of people, and I was beginning to feel cross. I couldn't afford to be delayed much longer. I had a busy fixed agenda in London, and those spare minutes I thought I had, had already been swallowed up sitting in Doncaster station. Anyway, what did 'considerably' mean?

As I thought about this, more people got on to the train, passengers from the York train who were being put on to ours. I looked up to see a wheelchair being placed across from me, for I was in the end section of the compartment which has space for wheelchairs. A pretty, bright-eyed little girl in the chair was chattering away to her companions, and soon we were a foursome, the little girl in her wheelchair, her big sister and her dad. Tina – for that was the girl's name – lost no time in telling me all the exciting things that had happened on her journey so far, that she was nine years old and was going to London. She and her family had started out very early indeed, much earlier than I had, from their home in the Yorkshire Dales, and I wondered why they had chosen such a day to take a trip to London.

Eventually the train started, much to Tina's delight. It made slow and sometimes non-existent progress, but the frequent stops only gave Tina more cause to look out of the window and excitedly and graphically describe to me what she could see. Then out came her 'dot to dot' puzzle book, and her 'Game Boy' – which was a complete mystery to me until she explained the finer points of it. We talked about her Brownie Pack, swapped stories of Brownie days – and she told me about her riding lessons and her love of animals. She got through several packets of crisps and a carton of orange juice, and then, returning to the subject of animals, asked me what my favourite animal was. 'Dogs,' I said, and her eyes widened with pleasure. 'Mine too, I'll draw you a picture of one to keep,' she exclaimed. In minutes she had produced a drawing of a happy-looking dog, coloured in and duly autographed, 'Love from Tina'. I did not have a chance to go through my papers, the minutes of the last meeting, to read my newspaper or even have a snooze, for Tina kept me one hundred per cent engaged.

Finally we arrived in London, the journey time extended by two and a half hours and both of us would be very late for our appointments. But her cheerful acceptance of the circumstances helped me to take the whole affair more philosophically than I might have done, had I been alone on the journey. Soon she was tucked up in her wheelchair, and with a cheery goodbye we parted company, heading for our important engagements, though I guess hers was far more important than mine. She was going to Roehampton Hospital in her wheelchair for a fitting for a new pair of legs, her present ones being carried by her dad in a large holdall. Tina had been born without legs – or arms either, apart from a short stump on her right shoulder. How did she write, draw, play games, open drink cartons and crisp packets? With her mouth, chin and use of that small stump. Her patience, courage and delight in life, coupled with an eager confident anticipation of the future, turned that delayed InterCity trip into a journey of discovery for me. I learned more from Tina that day than from any sermon, worthy book or important meeting. I got a glimpse through her eyes of what makes life really worthwhile, and of the pleasure to be had in the ordinary and in the unexpected. I experienced too the quiet courage of those who loved and cared for her, and who allowed her to be herself, rather than take her over. My instinct had been to open her crisps and drinks for her, to pass everything so she did not have to bend over or struggle, but I realised although that might have made the situation easier for me, it would have been wrong for her. She needed to do it for herself, and her dignity and her assurance were respected by those who had the wisdom to recognise her real need to be her own person.

The picture she drew for me that day I keep in the back of my diary, and when I get impatient with situations or frustrated by the actions of others, I look at that picture, and I reckon it helps me to get life a bit more in perspective. I may never meet Tina again, but I won't ever forget her, and I pray she will always 'walk tall' through life, though physically she cannot.

It was a good day, that snowy day in February. I gained so much, in spite of the delays, for it is not every day that one has the pleasure of meeting a young lady of such great distinction. A glimpse of the glory of God, travelling InterCity. It far outshone the luxury of first class; it was in a class of its own, a journey not measured in miles or time, but in eternal values, and with a glorious ultimate destination.

5

Through All the
Changing Scenes of Life

The rain had hardly stopped during the last few days. Winter seemed to have come with a vengeance, even though it was only the end of September. Then October came in the same, dark, dull and depressing. I felt sorry for the young couple whose wedding I was to conduct the next day, and at the rehearsal prayed that it would be a lovely day for them, in every sense of the word – weather included.

The morning of the wedding day did seem slightly brighter, as I drove over to the church to write up the registers and make sure everything was in order for the afternoon. I pushed open the door to be met by a blaze of colour, for the church was decorated for the harvest festival to be held that weekend. It was a feast for the senses, with the brilliant hues of flowers and foliage, the smell of fruit and vegetables mingling with the scent of flowers, and placed carefully along the sides of the sanctuary, the school children's harvest baskets. We had held the school's harvest thanksgiving the day before, and their baskets and decorations were still in place for the Sunday celebrations.

The churchwarden greeted me as I looked at the baskets. 'Shall I move them?' she asked.

'No', I said. 'They look lovely, and there's plenty of room for the bride and groom to walk through.'

She smiled at me. 'I'm glad you said that, I thought how nice they looked just there.'

When I returned to the church in the early afternoon the sun was attempting to break through. People were arriving for the wedding, chattering excitedly, their wedding finery vying with the harvest festival decorations. Having made sure the bridegroom and best man had arrived and were safely in place, and that the wedding rings were tucked away in the best man's pocket, I went to greet the bridesmaids who were standing nervously in the porch. I admired their dresses, checked the bride was on her way, then went back down the aisle, to find that the groom and best man had disappeared, leaving their top hats in the pew. A quick search revealed that they had been spirited off for a photo call, and they were back in place well before the bride appeared.

Soon a radiant bride was coming up the aisle on the arm of her proud father. I had told the bridegroom to turn and look at her, to welcome her, and as he did so I thought he was going to burst with pride and love. At that moment the sun shone through, lighting every inch of the church, and the people gathered there. The whole place seemed full of light and love, and as I stood there to conduct the service I too was bursting with joy – the presence of God was so real, God's love and human love filled that place. I looked out at the radiant scene before me, and I thought, 'Margaret, what a marvellous job you have got as a minister. God gives you all this to share with him, to touch lives at the most precious, deepest points – you are so fortunate.'

Later on in the service I was to lead that young couple, Andrew and Nicola, in their first walk together as husband and wife, to the altar, to pray for them and with them, and then see them going out into their new life, with family and friends supporting them – a new beginning, and God had given me the privilege of being part of it.

The next day was another golden day as I took into my arms a beautiful baby girl, and baptised her Annabelle Elizabeth Rosie, signing her with the sign of the cross, welcoming her into the Lord's family. Several years earlier I had shared in the marriage of her parents, Andrew and Allison, and been part of their special day; and here I was holding in my arms God's gift to them, baptising her 'in the name of the Father and of the Son and of the Holy Spirit'. I had seen Allison grow up. I knew all her family, for they were neighbours of ours. I was part of their family as a friend. I had shared in so many of their celebrations, and in a special unique way also as representing 'the Church' – Margaret, friend, neighbour and minister, sharing in the joy of new life, and being there to encourage that life, physically and spiritually to grow. What other job could give such joyous satisfaction?

During the following week I again waited at the church door where I had welcomed the wedding party the previous Saturday. The harvest decorations were still in place. This time it was not to welcome a bride but to bring comfort to those in mourning; to receive a coffin in which lay a lady who had spent her life in the village, a good long life lived out as a countrywoman, and now she came into church for the last time, her coffin covered in flowers. The church was filled with those who had come to say goodbye to a loved relative, a good friend, a respected neighbour; yet we could not be sad, it was an act of thanksgiving for a good, useful and long life. Now she was part of the 'harvest home'. We sang the hymn she had chosen for her funeral, 'O Jesus, I have promised to serve thee to the end'. She had kept her promise and God had kept his promise to her. Now she was at home with him, and together we thanked God for her life, and commended her to his care.

All in the space of a week I had shared in the three greatest points of life. In marriage, two people beginning a new life together as one. In baptism, the joy of welcoming a baby into the family of the Church. And in the last 'goodbye and thank you' for a long life which had come to its earthly ending.

Every baptism, wedding and funeral is different, because the people are different, yet in our community so many occasions are linked with one another. The very first wedding I conducted was of the granddaughter of a man I had got to know well during his last illness. In my frequent visits to him at home I hardly noticed the little granddaughter, I was more concerned with his wife, and the little girl's parents. Yet as that little girl grew up, fell in love and began to think about marriage, she was determined that I would be the one to conduct her wedding. At that time I was still a deaconess and unable to take weddings, although I assisted at many. Carolyn was adamant: 'When I get married, Margaret will take it.' So it was that soon after I was ordained deacon I was taking the wedding of

Carolyn and Glen. I don't remember who was more nervous, it was a toss-up between the bridegroom and myself. He kept asking me to go over the service with him beforehand, and I confessed to him, 'I'm nervous too, it's my first wedding you know, Glen,' to which he replied, 'Mine too, Margaret!' In the event all went well, and I have the video – and many happy memories to prove it.

Another wedding well remembered was when our daughter Alison was bridesmaid to her best friend, Lisa. I had plenty of pre-wedding briefing by my daughter on what and what not to say and do, and threats of what would happen if I made reference to their schooldays. I managed to refrain from doing so; I knew my place – after all, I was only conducting the ceremony, our Alison was the bride's best friend!

I have lost count now of the babies I have baptised, and yet the feeling of awe and excitement never diminishes, each time I take a child in my arms. As that child is handed to me I feel a very special bond between us. I know that many midwives feel the same about babies they help to bring into the world – that moment of new life, they are part of it, having a very important role. So it is for me as I look at the child I am holding. I often wonder what life will be like for that child. What will happen by the time they are eighteen, or twenty-one? What does life hold in store? I cannot answer those questions, no one but God can; but what I can do, and I do, is pray for that child and the family, commit them to the Lord, and pray they may all grow to know and love the Lord, and 'continue his faithful soldier and servant' as the Baptism Service says. Serving so long in one church and area

I do have the pleasure of seeing some of them growing up in the church, going through Sunday school,
being active in the life of the church, and now I
even have the children of former Sunday school
days, and former pupils of the village school,
bringing their children to be baptised. I suppose I
am a sort of spiritual grandmother – and it's not a
bad feeling at all!

As with baptisms I have lost count of the funerals
I have taken during my ministry so far. Some have
been of close friends, members of the church fellow-
ship, and of the local community. Often where
there has been a long illness before their death I
have built up very strong relationships with them
and their families, and again there has been that
awesome privilege and responsibility of being with
them through a very traumatic time, and still being
a shoulder to lean on afterwards. What always
touches me is the way people open their hearts and
lives at these times; they actually want me to be
part of their lives, there is a sense of acceptance. I
would never intrude, but wait to be invited – and
the invitations come. For that I am so grateful, as
then I can introduce them to my best friend who
can and will help them even more than any human
being, God himself. It's a matter of saying, 'Let me
introduce you to my friend, he has helped me, and I
know he wants to help you too.' There has to be
gentleness and sensitivity in doing this, with regard
for the vulnerability of those passing through suffer-
ing, grief and loss; and yet I would be failing them –
and God – if I did not bring the Christian message
into that situation. It has been said that 'there are
no atheists in a foxhole', and my experience tells
me that within every human heart there is a seeking

after the spiritual dimension, however it is expressed.

I am often struck, too, by their care and concern for me; I have been brought into their family circle, and I matter to them. This was brought home to me very powerfully just before my ordination to the priesthood. A man had suffered three bereavements in a very short passage of time, losing his aunt, mother-in-law and finally his wife. We had become closely involved through those times, although we had not known each other previously, and I did not expect that afterwards he would remain in contact, and yet he brought along a bottle of champagne for me, with the instruction that it was to celebrate my ordination to the priesthood, and put an extra sparkle into the celebrations. In his grief he was still concerned for my celebrations and wanted to add to them.

Ministry is not one-way; it is so often mutual, and it is in this meeting of lives, especially at what are known as 'rites of passage', that it is most deeply experienced. 'Rejoice with those who rejoice, and weep with those who weep' – to be allowed to do that, for me, is at the heart of my calling as a friend, and as a minister, and now even more so, as a priest. These are awesome, God-given, unique relation-ships, and all held together in the loving, healing and strengthening hands of God. 'Underneath are the everlasting arms', but God chooses to use human hands and arms to assist him as well – and that, for me, is the greatest wonder of it all.

6
For Everything There is a Season

Ten years in any job is a long time, and for ten years I had been Anglican Adviser to Yorkshire Television. It all began when they asked me to do a series of *Five Minutes* – a late night epilogue. This had led to other programmes, and to my being asked for advice on religious issues and such practical matters as what a bishop would be wearing at a harvest festival in *Emmerdale*, where to film a documentary on bereavement, which included a funeral, and who were the Church of England experts on such matters as racial issues and unemployment. When I was asked to succeed Brandon Jackson, the then Provost of Bradford Cathedral, as Anglican Adviser I felt both excited and scared. To follow such an experienced and talented man, and to be the first woman Anglican Adviser to an ITV company, would call for a great deal of energy and expertise; but with the blessing and the encouragement of the Archbishop of York, Dr Stuart Blanch, I took the plunge and accepted.

I was to join the well-known charismatic priest Monsignor Michael Buckley, who had become a much-loved television personality and who was the Roman Catholic Adviser, and Dr David Calvert, the Free Churches Adviser, who was a Methodist minister and an academic, who was able to draw out the deep theological issues and convey them so ably through television. We three were the Religious Advisers to the company, and during the years we were together we balanced each other in a good threesome, for we were friends and colleagues, and able to be a team as well as acting as individuals. We always used to say we were advisers, and did not bang any particular denominational drum – although we made sure our various denominations were well represented in the religious television output.

We were together in what I would describe as the heyday of religious television, and Yorkshire Television was at the forefront of the best of it. Series like *Sunday Best* with Donald Swann and Frank Topping, documentaries and features, as well as church services and epilogues, and a good link with news and current affairs, made those years some of the most exciting and rewarding I have known, not least for the wonderful and varied assortment of people in the television industry it was my privilege to know and work with. There were also the opportunities to learn about the industry, and how best to use and be used by it. When I was asked by the press early on how I saw my job, I said, 'I see my role as threefold: to advise on Christian matters, especially from the Anglican scene, to take part in programmes, and to care for the people I meet in YTV' – and that remained my aim during the years I spent as an adviser.

I was well used to radio, both local and national, and was convinced that the churches must be able to work with and in the media, including press, radio and television, for here were the opportunities to share the good news of Jesus Christ with those outside the Church as well as inside, not as 'hard sell', but to present the gospel in its many facets. To 'inform, educate and entertain' were the three hooks on which to present the ideas of faith, and I rated 'entertain' just as highly as 'inform' and 'educate'. Humour, music, drama, dance – these are all part of life, and life and faith are all of a piece to me.

As I read the gospels I see Jesus using so many different ways to touch people's lives for God. He used examples from life all around, and in the media age of today when people are so conditioned by images, fast-moving situations, colours and sounds, the gospel needs to be presented in the same idiom. After all, St Paul preached in the market place, John Wesley travelled round the country on horseback, the Salvation Army has its bands; what, I argued, was wrong with using television – reaching more people in one late night programme than a preacher in a church would reach in a lifetime?

If I was convinced, not everybody else was. During my time at YTV there were many people, including clergy, who took me on one side and said firmly, 'Margaret, are you sure you should be doing this? Is it right that you are spending so much time enjoying yourself, when there is so much need within the churches?' I thought long and hard about all this, and prayed hard too. I began to wonder whether they were right and I was wrong. It was true, I was enjoying myself; had it become an ego trip, or what? It was my fellow adviser, Michael Buckley, who helped me to make the decision. One day I asked him if he would give me some time to talk over with him what was happening, and whether it was right for me. I said, 'I want to talk with you not just as my friend Michael, or as my fellow adviser, but as a priest.' Michael spent time with me, listened and prayed, and with I believe godly wisdom and insight showed me I was in the right place, where God wanted me.

'All right,' I said at last. 'I know God wants me here, and he will keep me here as long as it is right. When he wants me out it will be equally clear.'

Ten years on, it was equally clear to me that it was time for out. I fought against it. Why should I give up something I enjoyed? Why now? I knew in my heart of hearts that I should. The television scene had changed, my two fellow advisers had gone their separate ways, Yorkshire Television had changed; and yet stubbornly I hung on, until one day I knew it was time to go, and I was going. Once I had made the decision I felt a great sense of relief, and I am sure some other people at Yorkshire Television felt the same – there had been clashes. Some felt I was too much the 'simple faith' type, and not enough concerned with theological issues. I was not an 'Anglican heavyweight' – though with tongue in cheek I might dispute that! At the end of 1990 Yorkshire Television and I parted company, over an excellent lunch and the presentation to me of an inscribed whisky decanter. On reflection I felt I should have left earlier, and yet God's timings are always right, and so it was to prove yet again.

Looking back, I thank God for the years at YTV, for opportunities, for experiences, and perhaps above all for real friendships made and maintained. I had always got on well with the *Calendar* team (news and current affairs) and in particular with the Head of Local Programmes, Graham Ironside, who always attended the Advisers' Meetings, the formal meetings when programmes were discussed, planned and appraised. I am a strong believer in the importance of getting religious issues into the general news output, and Graham too was a great supporter of this, and made sure religion was treated on equal terms with any other issue. A Scottish Presbyterian and a great newsman, I found in him an ally and friend, and that friendship has continued. I value what he wrote when I told him I was leaving YTV: 'Thank you for your enthusiasm and friendship, and for bringing a sense of enjoyment to every meeting we had . . .' Those words meant so much to me, and made up for some of the rough times I went through during my time there.

I had sought to keep my Christian integrity, and I hope my sense of humour, during those ten years, and I pray it was so. The lesson I learned was that, as it says in the book of Ecclesiastes, 'For everything there is a season, and a time for every matter under heaven . . . a time to keep and a time to cast away . . .' It is so easy to take up things – positions, opportunities, projects – but not so easy to give them up. Giving up seems like failure, and yet sometimes we have to let things go, to die to them, because the time is right. 'Turning the handle' on something just for the sake of it is not a right use of time, nor is it honouring to God, nor useful for the others involved. How many organisations, societies, meetings, efforts, in the church go on year in year out, which should have been given up or allowed to die, but those concerned have not been sensitive to the situation, realistic or, dare I say, humble enough, to let go? As someone said once with a wry smile – and a great deal of common sense: 'Much better people say "Why did he/she give it up?" than "Why didn't he/she give it up?" ' Learning to let go is as important as learning to take up. That goes for people as well as situations – and is maybe particularly relevant to parents and pastors.

'What are you going to do with yourself now?' was the general question I was asked when I said I was leaving YTV – as though I did nothing else! I came home on the day of the decision to find amongst my mail a letter which had been posted a couple of days previously. It was from John Nicholson, Chairman of 'Festival 92', which was to be a festival of Christian life and faith throughout the Leeds metropolitan area in 1992. All the main denominations had committed themselves to work together to demonstrate and proclaim the gospel at the start of the Decade of Evangelism, and the aim was to bring people to faith in Jesus Christ and discipleship within the Church, and also to demonstrate how Christians of diverse backgrounds could unite in that task.

John was writing to ask me if I would be one of the contributors, alongside the well-known evangelist J. John, who would be the main contributor, Roy McCloughry, Director of the Kingdom Trust and lecturer in social theology at St John's College, Nottingham, and Father Ian Petit, a Benedictine monk of Ampleforth Abbey, with vast experience of leading retreats and conferences both in the United States and this country.

I knew as I read the letter that this was what God wanted for me, this was the door he was opening, and this was why I needed to be free. Again, there was a wonderful sense of God's timing, and little did I realise then what an adventure it was going to be.

All I knew was that it was right, and my answer must be 'Yes'. I went back to the third chapter of the book of Ecclesiastes, those profound thoughts on time, and read again these words: 'He has made everything beautiful in its time . . .' Everything beautiful – ten years at YTV, Festival 92, life itself, God's beautiful arrangement of time – and I was part of it, praise the Lord!

7
Faith in the City

               I drove along the familiar route into Leeds, through the city and on to the road past Yorkshire Television. This time I did not turn right into the studios, but left, up past the forbidding-looking Armley Prison to an industrial park, finding, after some difficulty, a box-like unit, which had been lent to Festival 92 for an office. It was here I would meet those at the centre of the Festival, and J. John, the evangelist who would be spearheading it. My immediate reaction on meeting him was, 'I'm old enough to be his mother!' – and then, 'What have we got in common?' A good question, for certainly the answer to my first observation was correct age-wise. But what had I got in common with this swarthy young man with the flashing dark eyes? And what a strange name – J. John – it didn't sound like a real name at all. I was soon to find that his real name was quite unpronounceable, and the nearest was John John. A Greek Cypriot by birth, with a Mediterranean personality, he was 'all go'. A popular British evangelist, he has considerable experience of leading missions in many parts of the world, in cities and towns and with students – so he has a wide-ranging ministry.

     Looking round at the rest of the people gathered there, representing all the main denominations in the metropolitan area of Leeds, I came to the conclusion I had been asked as the 'token woman' – and maybe even the 'token older woman' – no doubt to counterbalance this young and swinging J. John. Those initial thoughts and anxieties were soon put to rest. Within minutes our ages, backgrounds and personalities mattered for nothing; we were instantly blended into the Festival 92 team. As the plans were unfolded I could see that this was going to be a major undertaking for me in terms of my time, but it was right, and if it was right then there had to be a one-hundred-per-cent commitment to it.

When I got back home I talked it over with Peter and then with my vicar, David, before putting it to our church. Many people are seconded to areas of mission overseas, or given leave for special projects, and I saw this in the same light. Yes, Leeds was only twenty miles away, but it was completely different from the area I lived and worked in. Festival 92 would be different also in that I would be working with all denominations, in churches and organisations quite unknown to me, throughout the city and its suburbs. It would mean a year's commitment, beginning in the autumn of 1991 through to the summer of 1992, when the whole project would culminate at Pentecost in a concentrated Festival in the centre of Leeds. A year for the city – and I dedicated that year, whatever it might bring. A dangerous undertaking, it would take every ounce of energy, but I knew it was right, and my family and church backed me.

Training sessions were held at different venues around the city in the autumn of 1991, so that Christians from the various churches could come together to get to know the Festival contributors, hear them speak and be trained in evangelism and counselling. The series was entitled 'Preparing the Ground', the three main sessions being 'Prayer and Purpose', 'Presence and Persuasion' and 'Power and Proclamation' – you could say all the 'p's' – and what is more it was 'p for people'. Watching them streaming in to attend these courses, their faces alight with eagerness, I could hardly believe this was part of what had been described as 'an apathetic and dying Church'. Here the Church was alive and well, and rolling up its sleeves for action, and I had the privilege of being part of it. I had given my word to the Festival organiser, a lovely and brilliant young lady, Rachel Trapnell, that invitations to speak or preach or lead meetings anywhere in the Festival area for the duration of the year would have priority in my diary – and the invitations poured in! Never in my life have I had such variety. There were fun days and festivals, open air meetings, Songs of Praise, coffee mornings, lunches, dinners, preaching here, there and everywhere, inside and out. In crowded churches and tiny meeting rooms, a full lounge in a sheltered housing block, a small group in a high-rise flat. With ethnic communities, or groups of disabled and handicapped people. Walks of witness, 'down by the riverside' services, flower festivals, concerts, exhibitions, prayer meetings, senior citizens' gatherings, young people's groups – you name it, I was there! Every tradition, every style of worship, and setting, was compressed into twelve glorious hectic wonderful months.

Much of the time I was on my own, as were the other contributors, for we each had our specialities. Mine was, I think, 'If they want me they can have me!' I had the time of my life; there was so much enthusiasm, such a desire to know more about Jesus and be committed to him. It was thrilling to hear people tell the story of their life freely and openly – and what lives many of them had led! They described situations I had never been through – so many had plumbed the depths, experienced tragedies, despair, feeling there was no hope or help, until they had met with Jesus and he had changed their lives; and what they were determined to do was share their good news with others. In quiet corners men and women sobbed their way into the kingdom of heaven, I saw the miracle of new birth before my eyes, and I could say, 'I was there.' The very special moments in personal conversation and prayer, the care and concern I was shown all went to make that year a tremendous one for me. 'Faith in the City' was no longer something I had heard about, but something I was part of, and I owe the Christians of the city of Leeds a great debt of gratitude for allowing me to share it with them.

We all came together as a team for the final week, both at St George's Church in the mornings with J. John and myself leading a series on 'Living Faith', and in the evenings at the Town Hall with all the team and guests led by J. John on the theme of 'Christianity Explored'. We were sure something marvellous was about to happen, that St George's and the Town Hall would be full to overflowing, hundreds would come to faith, and the life of the city and the churches would be renewed during that week – and it did not happen. Numbers were low, as compared to what had been happening when we went out to the various churches, and shared in their individual events. The Christians did not flock in, nor did the outsiders feel it was for them. What was meant to be the grand finale was very low key in numbers. J. John preached his heart out, and people did come to know Christ, but it was not on the scale that we had hoped and prayed would happen.

For those who had worked for so long to make the Festival a success there was sadness, frustration and disappointment. I shall never forget the final Friday morning as we sat in Canon David Hawkins' vestry at St George's Church, when someone said, 'Now I know how the Labour Party felt the morning after the election.' All the signs were good, everything pointed to full houses, full hearts and full lives, and in the end it was half measures, Christians had voted with their feet for some reason or other. Was it that they were afraid to come into the city, or too tired, or had other things on? Did they feel that, having had meetings all over the area with us going out to them, they had done their bit? Did their vision not stretch beyond their own patches? I don't know. Perhaps the thought of asking friends and neighbours to come to Leeds Town Hall to hear a preacher was too demanding, or maybe the style of the big rally is outdated.

The great climax went off like a damp squib. And yet over all I believe Festival 92 was a success, it was right to hold it, the seeds were sown, and in God's good time will come to fruition. Maybe our problem is that we live in an instant age; we want to see results now, we want growth now, we want to have it now. I know that the Lord is faithful, and however it may have looked in June 1992, the real story of Festival 92 will be known in the coming months and years, and some of it we will not know until we get to heaven.

Looking back on that hectic year I would not have missed a minute of it, especially being part of that wonderful team, and I thank God for the time of sharing, and witnessing, enjoying being with each other and being in the place we knew God wanted us to be – the exhilaration and the sheer delight of service.

Festival 92 is now 'water under the bridge' as they say, but I still feel sad for those who had the chance to be right in there and failed to seize their opportunity. Some words by Gavin Reid, Bishop of Maidstone, in a sermon around that time have remained with me, and constantly challenge me: 'If I have any fears for the future of Christianity in this country they rest not with the strength of outside opposition, but with the weakness of our inside commitment . . . the gospel is still the best news there is. We too have a gospel to proclaim . . . and there is no worthier cause given to human beings . . .' These words were part of a sermon he preached in Southwark Cathedral, London, for the Church Missionary Society. They hit the nail on the head for all of us who would call ourselves Christians, in cities or villages, town or countryside. Here we are now, half-way through the Decade of Evangelism. As I look around the churches I see very little sign of urgency, not too much enthusiasm to 'go and tell', so many just content to tick over in their faith and experience.

'The trouble with you, Margaret,' said a colleague to me one day, 'is that you want to drag people kicking and screaming into the kingdom of heaven, and it can't be done.' Yes I do, and not just kicking and screaming but praising, laughing, dancing, shouting. It can't be done? My reading of the gospel and my experience over and over again is that it can be done. 'Where there is a will there is a way' it is said. Once the Church finds its will, it will see the way. Jesus said, 'I am the way, the truth and the life' – what more do we need?

8
Vicar on the Move

It was one of those ordinary sort of days. David, my vicar, and I were having our staff meeting, mulling over what had been happening, sorting out the week and looking forward to getting on with the round of parish affairs; a very ordinary day indeed. Then suddenly David dropped his head and said very quietly, 'Margaret, do you think I should go?'

What was he talking about? 'What do you mean?' I demanded. 'Go where?' – although even as I said that I knew what he meant, for whenever David had something important to say he always dropped his voice and his head, almost as though afraid of the words and their consequence.

'Well, I've been thinking and praying a lot about it recently, whether it's right for me to stay here, or if it's time to go elsewhere. What do you think – tell me honestly.'

I was not prepared to discuss it before I had a chance to really think it through. 'Give me a few days, and we can both pray for wisdom in this, and then talk about it' I said.

We agreed to wait a few days, and then meet again to discuss it. It had come as a shock. Somehow I had imagined David would stay at St James' until his retirement. He had already been with us for twelve years, he was fifty-six, and had always said he would retire at sixty-five. He and Dorothy had made many friends, and a married daughter and her husband and two little grandchildren lived in York. We had often joked that we would spend all our years together at St James' and help each other up the aisle on our zimmer frames, propping one another up in old age. Although we laughed about it, it never occurred to either of us that things might change before we got to that state.

We were great friends as well as colleagues. It was a comfortable relationship, knowing each other's minds and ways. Yet as I thought about it I realised that David was right to be thinking about change. After twelve years he needed the stimulation of a new challenge. Maybe we had got into a rut – and ruts may be comfortable, but they are death traps, so easy to sink into but leading nowhere. The danger was that we could go on until either or both of us retired, and in our winding down so the church would wind down. It needed a fresh input, a new challenge and even stirring up.

I put these thoughts to David when we met. He nodded: 'Yes, I've been thinking along those lines too.'

'And if it's right for you to move', I went on, 'then you are going to have to get on with it now. After all, you will want to give at least seven or eight years to another parish.' We agreed that this was the time for him to begin to look around, but obviously not a word must be said to the parish or to anyone else. For the moment the matter was closed.

Over the next few months David and Dorothy looked at various possibilities. We did not mention them, but the unspoken acknowledgement was there. I even teased him about one or two of his treks away, but never pried. Early in 1993 he seemed edgy and ill at ease; one or two people remarked that he was not looking all that well, and it was evident that things were coming to a head. At last I suggested that we had better have a chat.

As we sat together, David looked far away. 'Right then, where and when?' I said firmly.

He looked startled: 'How did you know?'

I laughed. 'We know each other too well to keep secrets, don't we?'

Then he poured it all out, about the parish in East Sussex which they were sure was right, and they were going to accept. He grinned at me, looking much more his old self, 'I'm so glad I can tell you, it's been awful keeping it from you, although I think you knew something was afoot didn't you?' Excitedly he began to tell me about the new parish, and the people he had already met down there. As to when, it would be late summer, as they were hoping to have a new rectory by then.

Late summer – it was still early in the year, there was time enough to think about moving. But of course, once the decision had been made and accepted the parishes, both ours and theirs in East Sussex had to make the official announcement. I dreaded that announcement, for I knew how people would feel. So many relied on David, never thinking he would move. Now they would have to know he was going away, life was going to be different, there would be changes ahead, and that would be upsetting for many of them. The church stands for security in people's lives – sometimes it is the only security; and so change can seem very threatening and alien. Change a hymn book or the time of a service, even move the furniture around, and the objections come thick and fast. A new vicar – well, that spells change all right! But there was more to it than that. David and Dorothy had spent twelve years in the church, they were 'family', and just as when any family members move away it was like a bereavement, for although friendship remains, there will never again be that same close connection. David wrote about this in the Easter parish magazine: 'Dorothy and I are sure the decision is right, but that does not make it easy. These last nine months have been like living with a terminal illness, knowing the end will come, but not knowing when . . . Things will be tough in August when we start having to say goodbye to all the people we know . . .'

From then on everything had a degree of wistfulness and uncertainty. As we went through the annual festivals and events, each time I thought, 'This is the last time we will do this together.' Life in the parish seemed set 'on hold'. It reminded me of the time two years previously when my mother was very ill in hospital; we knew she was not going to get better, but how much time she had we did not know. One afternoon, driving back to Selby from the hospital in Cheshire, I was feeling very down, and switched on the car radio, hoping for something cheerful to brighten the journey – maybe a play I could lose myself in, or some music to take me out of myself. I found I had tuned into a programme about long-term illness, about the difficulties in that limbo state, and I almost turned it off, it was the last thing I wanted to think about. Then I heard a doctor speaking. His voice was calm and gentle, there was such warmth and understanding and compassion in it, and

I went on listening to him. He put into words how I was feeling, and finished by saying, 'The most distressing factor in all this is for the relatives; they can neither grieve nor hope . . .' That was it, but his actually saying it released in me all my pent-up feelings. I was glad to be alone, for I cried and sobbed as I drove, but as the tears fell so there came a great feeling of thankfulness and peace. Thankfulness for all the years I had had my mother, for all we had enjoyed as a family, all the fun we had shared, the fact she had seen me grow up. Thankfulness that she had seen Peter and me happily married, for the excitement of the arrival of two grandchildren, and of watching them growing up into delightful adults who showed her and their granddad such love and affection. Thankfulness that my parents had enjoyed their diamond wedding celebrations, for the sharing, the loving and the laughter. Then the peace, knowing that she was in the hands of God who loved her, and who would care for her, even more than we could.

I thought of what she had said just a day or two before, with her great sense of humour: 'I'm ready to go. When it comes to someone having to wipe your behind for you, it's time for off . . .' Of talking to her about heaven, and my saying, 'Well, you've lots of friends in heaven, Mum, there's So-and-so and So-and-so, and . . .' She had looked at me, with that stern look she gave when I'd failed to grasp the point of a remark. 'There are NO strangers in heaven – they are all friends!' she told me firmly. I knew soon the time would come when we would grieve, but now we would make the most of each day, each visit, each chance to show our love, for we had been given this time together. What about hope? In one way, no, Mum was not going to get back to full health and vigour; but the hope we had was sure and certain, the hope of eternal life. She was going on ahead, and would be there to welcome us home one day, just as she had always stood at the door to welcome us. She had hated growing old, with the restrictions that age brought, she resented the grey hairs and wrinkles – 'I look in the mirror and see an old woman, and I don't like it!' – how could we grieve for her? I thought of the words from Isaiah 40: 'They who wait for the Lord shall renew their strength, they shall mount up with wings like eagles, they shall run and not be weary, they shall walk and not faint.' Mum was waiting for her wings, soon she would fly – as one day we would too. On the drive back that afternoon God had got the message through to me, through a voice on the radio, and through his word. That sense of thankfulness and peace continued, and has remained, and I pray always will.

The last few months David was our vicar were busy. There seemed so much to do, so many ends to tie up, so many goodbyes. One of the great joys for him and for all of us was that in our village church at Wistow, with the Methodist chapel standing right opposite, the two congregations had at last come together, officially united as a Local Ecumenical Project. I remembered the first time I had gone to take a service at the church, over twenty years before, and had parked my car near the chapel, only to be told by a very stern-looking gentleman that 'church folk park that side', pointing to the other side of the road. Thankfully those days had gone, and over the years the church and chapel had drawn closer together, sharing so much of their life, until the time came when they voted to become one, still retaining both Methodist and Anglican forms of service, but sharing together in worship, and in their life together. David and his Methodist minister colleague Patrick got on so very well, and of course this made such a difference.

The Methodist minister left about the same time as David, in fact they had a joint leaving party and presentation at Wistow, and Patrick was succeeded by a woman Methodist minister. I was delighted to have a female colleague there, and as I said at the time, 'They say two women cannot get on in the same kitchen but Marian and I certainly get on in the same patch' – and we continue to do so.

It was a year of comings together, for in our village of Camblesforth where we live the Methodists and Anglicans had also covenanted to work together as one, based at the chapel. The Methodist minister, Julia, and the vicar, John, and I had been working together for several years in the village, each taking services as well as the local preachers, and it was a natural and happy decision to put this on a formal footing, to be 'the church in Camblesforth'. It is often said that it is more difficult in villages, they find it harder to adapt to change. For the villages of Wistow and Camblesforth it proved quite the opposite. Of course, not everyone welcomed change, and it will take a long time to achieve the hopes and prayers made at the covenant services, but the will is there, the acceptance of 'better together'. Growing together is like growing up, there's unevenness, pain and stress at times, it is not always fun, but it is worth it in the end. Jesus said to his friends, 'This is my commandment, that you love one another as I have loved you.'

Keeping that in our hearts and minds, and by his grace putting it into practice, means that, in the words of the old British Rail slogan, 'We're getting there!'

So 1993 was a year of changes, of comings and goings, of uncertainties and sadness, and yet of knowing that God had it all in hand, that he had blessed us, and would bless us, in the future as in the past. It was a small girl who brought that fact home to me in a very special way, reminding me that the words 'a little child shall lead them' are equally true for today as in the time of the prophets.

I had been taking the usual Friday morning school assembly at Wistow, we had sung our final song with great gusto and the children had trooped back to their classes, except for one small girl. She held her song book in her hand: 'Mrs Cundiff, why do you always sing "He's got the whole world in his hands", because it doesn't say that in the book, look!' She held out her book to me and underlined a word with her finger. 'It says hand, not hands!'

I had to admit I hadn't realised that.

She went on, 'So if God has got the whole world in his hand, what is he doing with his other one?'

There is a deep question for a Friday morning! I thought fast. 'He holds the world in one hand, and blesses it with the other, one underneath, the other above.' I gave her a demonstration with my hands.

She brightened up. 'Oh yes, that's nice isn't it?' and with that she was off to join her classmates.

I stood there holding Lucy's song book, thinking about what I had just said. I had a clear picture of God, holding not just the world, but all of us, safe and secure, and a hand extended over us in blessing, shielding us, protecting us. Above us, beneath us, with us, for us. A great spiritual truth – but it had taken a small girl to bring it home in a very personal and new way that morning.

As I walked out across the playground, I was humming a tune – no prizes for guessing what it was!

9

The Space Between

After the initial reaction when David announced he would be leaving, the parish settled down almost as though nothing had happened. After all, 'late summer' was a long time ahead, and there were holidays and visitors and all sorts of things happening, there would be plenty of time to think about it later. For David and me there was a lot to be done. We looked at the situation realistically and estimated that there would be at least a six-month interregnum, which would take us well into the new year. Now was the time to be booking up clergy to take the Holy Communion services at both St James' and Wistow. David made a large chart, and gradually he was able to fill in a lot of the spaces. For me it was a time of frustration. 'If only I had been ordained priest by now we wouldn't need to do all this', went through my mind over and over again. The congregation began to notice the problems we would face, and it began to dawn on them as late summer got nearer that we were going to be very reliant on other local clergy who were busy themselves anyway. Fortunately there were one or two retired clergy also who were willing to take quite a number of services, but they had to travel in to Selby, and it would be at the worst time of year, from autumn onwards.

I felt as though I had my hands tied behind my back; there I was, but unable to do more than assist. Added to this, our very able and popular Reader, Colin, had to move to London because of his work, and so I would not have him as a colleague and support during this time. But never mind the future, and our anxieties, we were all determined that David and Dorothy's leaving party would not be a sad affair. 'No tears,' I said firmly. 'It is a celebration and thank you for the years we have enjoyed together, not a wake!'

It was a celebration, as we were able to say 'thank you' for those years we had all shared together, but on the last Sunday there were many tears. It was hard for all of us, especially David and Dorothy, to get through the final services. David confessed to me a couple of days before they left that he would have liked to have run away, and not to have had to face the goodbyes, but they had to be said, and the tears had to flow.

It was with heavy hearts that we closed the church door that night. A chapter of life was ending, and we had no idea of what would be written in the next one. A few of us made the journey down to Northiam in East Sussex for David's licensing. It is a beautiful part of the country, the old church was bright and sparkling to welcome the new rector, the people were excited and welcoming, and we could see that they had already taken David and Dorothy to their hearts. Yet we felt outsiders, and we were. We were part of the past, not the present. It was quite hard to listen to the speeches of welcome, with David described as 'our new rector'; as one lady who had made the journey down from Selby said afterwards, 'I wanted to say "That's our Vicar" – but of course he wasn't ours any more.'

Summer gave way to autumn, then winter. Life went on, it had to. People began to rally round. After a few initial hiccups a pattern evolved. The wardens got into their stride, and rose to the demands of the office. Sean, a young man coping with a debilitating illness, and Jean, a shy widow, had no previous experience of an interregnum but found themselves doing things they would have never imagined they were capable of doing. They discovered anew that the Lord does give the strength and the wisdom to those who are willing to step out in faith and service. These were long, hard months, but neither would have missed the experience – though as they both say, they would not like to go through it again for a few years! Seeing them getting on with the extra work load inspired others to take a greater share in the life of the church, realising we were all in it together. The same was true at Wistow. The small congregation rallied round Diana and Joan, the wardens, and together with their Methodist counterparts enabled the United Village Church of Wistow to continue with its worship pattern and witness, and its care of the community. I found it very heart-warming the way they were concerned for me, not demanding more of my time, but seeking how they could help me with the work. Their response was always, 'Leave it to us, love, we'll see to it!' But I still felt very sad and inadequate that I was not able to help them more.

If only I had been ordained priest by now it would have relieved the pressure on other clergy who had to come in to be the celebrants at the Holy Communion services, not only in the two churches but in the various places where we took Communion in the parish, and for individuals at home. For me, it was like seeing people holding out their hands for food, and my having in my hands the food they needed yet being held back from giving it to them. I have never felt so frustrated in all my ministry as during that time of interregnum. I found it hard going, and yet I can look back now and see how much I learned through it. I like to be able to do what is needed, to meet every need, and feeling powerless does not come easy to me. There is still within me the child who was so sure she was going to change the world single-handed when she grew up – and it is a hard lesson to learn that I am mortal, frail, inadequate and restricted!

I was talking to the former Archdeacon of York, Leslie Stanbridge, one morning. 'How are you getting on then, Reverend Mother?' he asked, a title he had bestowed on me some years back in his humorous way.

'My main problem is Christmas morning,' I moaned. 'Who is going to come out to Selby to take a service Christmas morning?'

'What time do you want me?' came the direct reply.

'Oh, you don't want to trail out to Selby on Christmas morning . . .'

Leslie broke in, 'That was not the question. I asked what time you wanted me.'

'Nine thirty?'

'I'll be there' said Leslie – and he was. Help was available if I would ask for it – the trouble with me is that I do find it difficult admitting I need help, but God has his own way of getting the message across to me, not least during an interregnum!

During that time the situation regarding the Communion services and who actually did what dawned on many members of the congregation. While David and I had worked together we had shared all the services, including the Holy Communion of course, and perhaps few realised what was done by the priest alone. But it was always David who pronounced the absolution, who said the prayer of consecration and gave the blessing. As the deacon I took most of the service, and shared in the preaching and administration, but our roles were different, even if not obviously so. With visiting clergy I always stood back, as I believed was right; it was my job to fit in with them and not them with me, and I was happy to have it so, but members of the congregation remarked about the change. 'I felt so cross, Margaret, seeing you stand to the side and that man take over . . .' said one lady, very annoyed, one morning, while another commented, 'I felt sad seeing you side-lined.' I had to explain that I had not been pushed out or side-lined at all, I was a deacon; it was just that David and I had been able so to order the services that it had not been too noticeable. So maybe it was a good thing that it did raise in people's minds what the issue of the ordination of women to the priesthood was about. Perhaps they began to understand that priesthood is not just to do with 'being in charge' but with being able to serve more fully.

Looking back now I see what a busy year it was in so many ways, not just in the parishes, with the round of services, baptisms, marriages, funerals, visiting, teaching and all the rest that goes to make up the parochial ministry; but in travelling, writing, broadcasting, preaching. Such variety! My engagements outside the parish included preaching in the chapel at Emmanuel College, Cambridge; giving one of the York Cathedral Lectures entitled 'Good News, Fact or Fiction? The Gospel and the Media'; leading a week at Scargill House; speaking at various conferences, and attending the Diocesan Communications Officers' Conference in Strasbourg and the Diocesan Clergy Conference at 'Funcoast World' in Skegness – besides numerous committee and council meetings. Life was neither dull nor quiet. Being one of the judges for the Religious Television Awards for the Sandford St Martin Trust under the chairmanship of Monica Sims made the communications adrenalin run, and stimulated my mind to think afresh about the place of religious television. It is said that 'variety is the spice of life' – life had plenty of spice that year!

One issue, though, dominated that time. The probability that ordination to the priesthood was now only a year away, was so awesome a thought that I could hardly take it in. I do not now regret that waiting period, for what it did more than anything during that time of interregnum was to confirm even more strongly my sense of calling to priesthood. As I look back at the things that have happened over the years, even in the more public and exciting events of my life, I see shot through everything the clear, steady confirmation of God's calling. Waiting was hard, but the end was in sight, it was going to happen!

Something else was going to happen too; we were to have a new vicar the following February. He came, he saw, he liked, we liked – it sounds so simple, and in a way it was. Early in December we met for the first time, sat and talked together not just about the parishes but sharing ourselves, our expectations and fears, what we hoped for in the future and our realisation that the future for both of us was a step into the unknown. We did not know where it would lead either of us eventually. Strangers we were, maybe even a bit wary of one another, and yet I sensed that somehow our lives were going to be very much interwoven in the future.

He had already gained 'Brownie points' in my estimation: he had a delightful wife, Audrey; they were from the west country – their home at Crowcombe in Somerset was but a stone's throw from my old family home in Dunster – a small world indeed; and they had two adorable and friendly dogs.

Later in the day I talked to Michael our treasurer, who had also met David (yes, another David!) and Audrey that morning. We decided we had liked what we saw.

'Only one thing,' said Michael gloomily, 'He's got dogs!' – Michael is not known as a dog lover.

'Oh yes, dogs,' I replied cheerfully. 'That's good, I can always get on with people who like dogs.'

Michael winced, and then grinned at me in his Michaelish way. 'Ah well, if he is God's man for this place then we'll have to put up with the dogs.'

'Dogs,' I thought to myself dreamily. I was already looking forward to what lay in the future, with new four-legged friends, and of course their two-legged owners! Life had suddenly taken a turn for the better!

10
'The Time Has Come . . .'

All of a sudden, or so it seemed, the road to priesthood was opening wide. Hurdle after hurdle was being cleared, in spite of all the rumblings, and although I had hardly dared hope, it was now almost a certainty. The question was not now 'if', but 'how' and 'when'. So it was a great relief and delight to receive a letter from the Archbishop of York, spelling out the possibilities, and what would need to be done.

The opening words, 'Dear Margaret, The time has come to let you know about the plans being made in this diocese for the ordination of women deacons as priests . . .' made my heart and my spirit leap, and as I read the letter, with great thanksgiving, I thought too of so many of my friends in the diocese, in the same position as myself, opening their letters, and of the joy they would all be feeling. The Archbishop outlined the progress of the legislation, the fact that it had to be debated by both Houses of Parliament in the November of 1993 – a year on from the Synod vote. Then had to come the Royal Assent, and finally, if all that went through, the hope was that the new Canon would be ready to promulgate – proclaim officially and finally – on Tuesday, February 22nd, 1994, at a special meeting of the General Synod.

No ordinations could of course take place before then, so it was likely to be around Easter that the first ones could take place. Before then, there was the inevitable paperwork, meetings and interviews, reports on candidates for priesthood. We were asked to think and pray about our response, whether we wished to offer ourselves and to discuss this with our colleagues and congregations. We were to get in touch with our Suffragan Bishop – in my case, the Bishop of Selby – who would plan interviews and make the preparations to meet with potential candidates. In his usual very clear and concise manner, the Archbishop had spelled out all the formalities and possibilities, answering the many questions that would naturally arise. As I came to the end of a very detailed letter my heart made another leap, for there in black and white were the dates for the ordinations:

> We therefore propose to hold two Ordination Services in the Minster on two successive Saturday mornings, May 14th and May 21st. Candidates from the East Riding Archdeaconry and the Eastern half of the Cleveland Archdeaconry will be ordained on May 14th by the Bishop of Hull, and those from the Selby Archdeaconry and the Western half of the Cleveland Archdeaconry will be ordained on May 21st by the Bishop of Selby . . .

The words, 'on May 21st by the Bishop of Selby' shot off the page like golden arrows: those few formal words took my breath away. There was an actual date, a point in time set aside, a date that embedded itself in my heart and in almost all my waking thoughts that day. I took out my 1994 diary, and wrote in under May 21st, 'Possible ordination to the priesthood'. I looked at what I had written, and somehow seeing it actually written there brought home to me that a momentous time lay ahead. Yet I dared not write 'ordination to the priesthood'. 'Possible' it was, but there was still a long haul ahead, and anything could happen. God had brought me this far, it was in his hands and for me it was a matter of 'one step at a time'. 'Best foot forward then', I said to myself as I put away my diary. 'Take it as it comes.'

The next development came almost at once, in the form of a letter from the Bishop of Selby. He wrote to say that the planning towards the ordination as priests of women who were already deacons was now going forward. He had asked the Reverend Margaret Escritt to assist him in the reviews, and he would like me to help also. I knew Margaret well, we had first met over twenty years ago. She had been a parish worker before she had married the Archbishop of York's chaplain, Michael Escritt. They moved just across the road from the Palace when Michael became Vicar of Bishopthorpe, where they were for eleven years before they came to Selby in 1983, when Michael was appointed Vicar of Selby Abbey. Margaret worked as a chaplain at a York hospital, and then became Diocesan Adviser for Diaconal Ministries. She was ordained deacon in 1987, at the same time as me, and when she and her husband moved to York she was appointed to work part-time in another parish there and also as an assistant chaplain at Full Sutton Prison; so she has a wide-ranging experience of ministry. Like me she is also a Bishops' Selector for the Advisory Board of Ministry, which means we are part of a team who assess men and women offering themselves for ministry.

We were both well used to meeting candidates for the ordained ministry, but this was rather different. Now we were being asked to help the Bishop in discerning vocation to the priesthood in those who were already deacons. In fact, many of them had been parish workers and deaconesses for years before that, and it could be thought that of all people they had a right to be ordained priests – their commitment and service showed that. However, this was a new situation, unique in fact, and the House of Bishops had set out guidelines to be observed:

> Ordination to the priesthood should not be regarded as an automatic right. A Deacon whose vocation to the priesthood is accepted after a process of discernment may recognise this as a positive affirmation of that vocation by the Church . . . The process should acknowledge the previous selection, training, experience and ministerial standing of the Deacon, recognising that many women deacons had been in ministry for a number of years, and were not originally selected for ordination to the priesthood.

What it came down to for us was that each candidate would meet with either Margaret or myself, and also with the Bishop. It meant too that Margaret and I interviewed each other, and were also interviewed by the Bishop – so we went through exactly the same procedure as everyone else. We may have been assisting the Bishop, but we were also deacons coming forward for our vocations to be tested.

As I look back on that time, I count myself very privileged to have been part of that whole process, which was so affirming of us as individuals, as Christians and as ministers. To sit down, in relaxed surroundings, at the Bishop's house, and to be able to talk with him and with a fellow deacon about the past – the failures as well as the successes; to look at our lives as they were, at the ministry we were involved in, how we saw our future ministry, our hopes and fears; to be able to express our anxieties, our sadnesses, our excitement and our experience of God's calling, up to the step which had brought us to this point; all this was, I found, humbling yet affirming. It was a releasing of so much of myself which could have been painful and frightening, had it not been that I knew I was in a prayful, caring, loving and welcoming situation. I suppose in a way it was being with 'soul friends'. I did not need to hold anything back, but could be totally free, knowing that God had brought me to this time, this place. He was there, and there need be no fear. It was again an experience of what the old hymn says: 'Count your blessings, name them one by one, and it will surprise you what the Lord has done.'

Going through the process as a candidate was very helpful, and I was glad to have had that time. I found it a deeply spiritual experience, and I am convinced it helped me as I then became one of those with the responsibility of sharing in the review. Each person had her own story to tell, and each one was different. They had all come by their own individual pathway, each one responding to God's call to service. As I listened, I marvelled at the wealth of experience, the variety of ministry, the sheer guts and 'stickability' of these women.

Shot through each story was that golden cord of obedience and faithfulness. Their stories told of hardship and adventure, of times of darkness and uncertainty, as well as of doors of opportunity that had opened up. Sometimes they had been able to use their gifts and abilities to the full, and had had the joy of seeing so much accomplished in the place where God had set them.

What I also found was that not one was resentful about the past, or would have changed her path. 'With hindsight, would you have done the same?' I asked. Some looked at me in sheer amazement that I had asked such a question. Not one said, 'I wish I had done something different,' or, 'If I had known it would have been so long . . .' They did not begrudge the years they had given so freely, and now they offered themselves afresh to be used in God's service, to the Church and to its people, asking that their vocation to the priesthood might be tested.

One of the main questions asked was, 'How long before we hear?' We had all waited so long already that it was hard to bear this final period of waiting. But the Bishop was well aware of our feelings. Christmas was almost upon us and there would be an inevitable delay in official letters reaching us. In his gracious and loving way, he told each one of us individually that he was prepared to recommend us for ordination, and in due time we would hear from the Archbishop. What a Christmas present! No Christmas lights shone as brightly as did our faces when we heard the news, no carol was sung with as much happiness as the song of thankfulness we sang in our hearts. 'Merry Christmas and a Happy New Year' – merry in the nicest possible way. And the new year? It was going to be a year to remember!

Towards the end of January came the official letter from the Archbishop of York: 'Dear Margaret, I am writing to you on the recommendation of the Bishop of Selby to confirm my willingness to accept you for ordination to the priesthood . . .' Then followed a list of dates, for the Ordination Service itself, and the rehearsal, and for the preparation course and Ordination Retreat to be held beforehand. His letter concluded:

This is a bare statement of the arrangements for an event which, I hope, will bring you great joy and blessing in the days ahead, and which will enrich the ministry of the whole Church as you bring your gifts to be used in the service of our Lord in this more extended ministry. May God bless and guide you as you prepare to receive his grace for the work that lies ahead. Yours sincerely, John Ebor.

I read again those words, 'as you bring your gifts . . .' What were my gifts? I could do many things. I prided myself on my ability to deal with certain situations and people. I had been trained in the art of communications. I had learned through experience how to cope with many and varying complicated affairs. I knew the 'nuts and bolts' of administration. I had been on courses for this, that and the other. I knew how to open my mouth at the right time, and to keep it shut at others, although sometimes I got the two things mixed up! I had a sense of humour, and I liked people – well, most people. I could express my faith easily, was not put off by opposition – rather the opposite, I could dig my heels in when I felt it necessary.

But were these gifts enough? I knew they were not, and I was also conscious of my failings and inadequacies. What had I got to offer? I loved God, I trusted in Christ, I knew a strength and power beyond myself, the power of the Holy Spirit at work in my life, in spite of my many mistakes. I had a strong and abiding sense of calling to priesthood which had grown over the years. But these were God's gifts to me, not mine to him. Some words came into my mind as I read the Archbishop's letter, words I had sung many times over the Christmas period:

What can I give him, poor as I am?
If I were a shepherd, I would bring a lamb;
If I were a wise man, I would do my part;
Yet what I can I give him –
Give my heart.

The only gift worth offering was my heart – me, one hundred per cent: 'Here you are, Lord, here's me, it's all I have got, but I'm yours to use as you decide, wherever you put me, whatever happens.' God's gift to the Church? Yes I am, just like all the others who have offered themselves in service. We have many and varied gifts, all of us, and Jesus intended it that way. He said, 'Follow me,' and there have always been those who have responded, who have been prepared to step out in faith with him. All sorts of people – and somehow the Church has gone on growing. More and more have been brought in, have discovered something of the glory of God, and of their calling to share him, and have gone out to others with that good news of the glory of God, seen in Jesus, experienced by the Holy Spirit.

'The whole Church,' the Archbishop said, and that transcends denominations. It means the body of Christ, his Church, since the day he first called men and women to join him in the greatest adventure of all time, with his power to be his people, and to bring others into his kingdom. I had been part of all that ever since the day I committed myself to him as a teenager, all through these years, and now it was time to take 'one more step' into the glorious privilege of further service. Yes, 1994 was going to be quite a year one way and another, and I meant to enjoy every minute of it!

11
Be Prepared!

He bounded in, a man used to striding over the fells, tall and cheerful, with a boyish grin which belied his fifty-five years. David Woollard had arrived! As I stood in the vestry of St James' Church, where I had been part of the furniture and fittings for well over twenty years, I thought back to the last service of its kind held here, in October 1980 when David Bond had been instituted and inducted as vicar. I remembered his coming through that same vestry door quietly and rather nervously, and my wondering how we would get on together. Get on we did, for almost thirteen years, during which time we had not only shared in the ministry, but in our lives, our family situations, our worries and our joys. We had prayed and worked together, helped each other through difficult situations, cried on each other's shoulders at times, and laughed together a lot as well. We were at ease with one another, we had grown together, and all the big decisions in our lives we discussed with one another, valuing each other as friends and companions on the same road.

Now here was another David – 'Not Mark 2', I told myself firmly, 'he will be himself.' He might bear the same Christian name, but in all other respects he was very different. His background, his experience, his interests, his roots, his journey of faith; all these and more had made him the person he was. He had trained at a different theological college from the last three vicars of St James'. They had all been 'old Oaks' from Oak Hill College in London, but our new vicar had studied at Trinity College in Bristol, before coming to York as a curate, first at Clifton parish church, and then at St Luke's. Our previous vicars had all come from other dioceses, this David had spent all of his ministry – a mere five and a half years – in York diocese. There was one thing in common, though, with the last three vicars; it had been their first livings, and was David's first too. He had spent his working life in a variety of occupations before following his calling to the ordained ministry, so now coming to be vicar of his own parishes, here at St James' and All Saints', Wistow, would give him the chance to lead in his own way.

So here he was – our new vicar. How would it work out? I had done a lot of hard thinking and praying about my own future during the last year or so. Was I too much of a fixture at St James'? Was it right for the parish, for a new vicar, or for me, for me to remain here? Something my husband had said during the interregnum had remained in my mind, and challenged me to think about the future. We had been talking about the parish and I had said cheerfully, 'Well, St James is an attractive proposition, I shouldn't think there will be any trouble filling it,' to which Peter had replied quietly, 'Don't take this wrong, love, but maybe some men might be put off with you being there.' I bristled a bit, but realised what he was saying. After all, old fixtures and fittings can hamper progress, can get in the way, can even prove a stumbling block. I had seen it happen in other places and I did not want my being at St James' to detract from the life and growth of the church, or to be any sort of a brake on new ideas and actions. A new vicar needed to be able to do things in the way he felt right, and not to have to look over his shoulder.

So I had begun to think that maybe it was time for me to ease away from St James'. I was now heavily involved with the ecumenical project in my own village, not just with services but in pastoral work. I was also an honorary chaplain at York Minster for a day a month, and I was much in demand as a speaker and preacher both within the diocese and outside. Added to this was my work in communications, in writing and broadcasting – and I was not getting any younger! Then there was the new dimension of being ordained priest later in the year. How would this work out with a new vicar? I realised as I thought about these things that they were for 'the third time of asking'. I had experienced three interregnums whilst I had been at St James', and as each new vicar had been appointed the same thoughts – or many of them – had gone through my mind, not least, 'Will we get on together?'

For me as a non-stipendiary minister with outside work too, this was not so great a problem as for women in full-time paid ministry. As assistants they were in a difficult position when there was a change of vicar. He might not want them; maybe they would not get on together, and he could have someone else in mind he wanted to bring in. There was no security of a continuing ministry for a woman. I can think of many women I have known who have gone through agonies in this situation. They have been, or have felt, pushed out. For many single women, where the parish had become their home and family, having to move was very traumatic indeed; in effect, a bereavement, having to start all over again, with the knowledge that it could all happen again in similar circumstances. I had been fortunate so far, and it had worked out, but times had changed, as well as vicars. Maybe the time had come . . .

I looked across at David. He was obviously excited, full of 'get up and go' enthusiasm as he was beginning his new ministry here. I wanted the very best for him and for the church. As for me – well, I could leave that to God; no doubt it would all be revealed in time. Now it was time to rejoice that God had provided David for us, to praise him for the answer to our prayers and to pray for David and his family as they took this new step in their lives.

David grinned across at me: 'Right, let's go!' And so off we went, singing

Tell out, my soul, the greatness of the Lord!
Unnumbered blessings give my spirit voice;
Tender to me the promise of his word –
In God my saviour shall my heart rejoice.

As the service of Institution and Induction began, and we welcomed David as our vicar that February night, there began a new chapter in all our lives.

During the next few weeks we began to get to know each other, sounding one another out, sorting out patterns of worship and meetings, filling in the background to the parish and area. The first big change came within a week.

'Would you mind if we swapped stalls? You have the vicar's one and I'll have yours.'

I hesitated, wondering what all this was about. It seemed a strange move.

'Why?'

David laughed. 'Well, it's the overhead projector screen that swings across. With me being so tall it's likely to take my head off, you fit underneath it!'

'Done,' I said. 'We don't want the vicar be-headed, do we?'

We quickly found ourselves making other adjust-ments; nothing to do with our height – or lack of it – but finding out how each other tackled situations, looked at problems, handled the everyday things of parish life. I soon discovered he was a very ob-servant man. He was chatting away one morning about an idea he had when he suddenly stopped in mid-flow. 'You don't agree with that do you?' he said, rather anxiously, 'I can tell by your face.'

I realised I had been deep in thought, and often when I am thinking I tend to frown. 'Don't worry about that, it's my thinking face,' I told him. He looked relieved. So that was all right.

It made me realise, though, how much we do convey by our expressions, what is popularly known as 'body language', and that here was a man who was very sensitive to signs, to the responses of others, because he cared. He was concerned about how I felt about the future, and what I wanted to do. I didn't want to rush into anything; it was early days yet, and with priesthood coming up I wanted to adjust to one thing at a time. I realised I was feeling very relaxed about the future; somehow it did not seem to matter. I had imagined I might have been feeling quite uptight by now, and yet the reverse was true. Some words came into my mind, 'the peace that passes all understanding'. Yes, that was it! I did feel at peace; there was a sense of rightness, of acceptance and of safety, like being enveloped in warm sunshine.

Sunshine was very much the order of the day as on a glorious spring morning in March I drove to our Diocesan Retreat House, Wydale Hall, near Scarborough. Those of us to be ordained priest in the diocese had been called to attend a four-day course on 'Preparing for Priesthood', and I had been looking forward to it with a mixture of excitement and apprehension. What was going to happen? Would there be any space to think? Would I be able to shut my door and relax at all? As I joined the rest of the members of the course I realised what a varied lot we were, from some in their early thirties, several of whom had brought their babies with them, through all the age range to over seventy. And such variety of ministry and experience! Here we were together, at the same point in our lives. In just a few weeks' time we would all be ordained priests, enabled to serve God more fully in the Church. But what is a priest? What were we going to be? Did we really know? We teased out thoughts, words and ideas, we came up with lists and expressions. But did they convey what we really felt?

It was hard going the first two days as we began to open up and be opened up to ourselves. Some found it very painful as the many hurts, frustrations and anxieties came to the surface. I sensed that for some who had gone through very difficult times they had never been able to let those experiences go, they were almost superglued to them. But now in the prayerful supportive company of fellow candidates they could let go, and be themselves. They felt safe to express their innermost feelings. I have to admit that I found this a very difficult time. I had set out for the course full of joy and anticipation, grateful to God and the Church that I was privileged to be accepted, and I found it difficult to cope with some of the negative things that were being so forcefully expressed. I found myself feeling resentful that in a way my joy was being diminished by it all.

It was not until the end of our four days together that I realised how important that time had been for all of us; for us all to be free together, freed to serve one another – to put into practice the words of St Paul to the Galatians, 'Bear one anothers' burdens and so fulfil the law of Christ.' It was evident that many of those burdens had been recognised, lifted and disposed of because of our corporate sharing, and looking back now I realise how valuable and liberating it was for all of us. What is a priest? We discovered something of that in a practical way during our time together that week.

There was fun, too, not least in one session which was called 'Looking after the Priestly Personage', when a most elegant lady spelled out the need for us to look after our bodies, and gave us information on how to avail ourselves of the latest in sporting and beauty establishments. I had visions of myself trying out these various activities, remembering school days when I never even managed to climb the wall bars or get over the horse in the gym! I am afraid the mental picture reduced me to tears of laughter, and it was evident that others were remembering their own inadequacies also; to which our speaker responded firmly, 'You have only one body, you will not get another, it's up to you to look after it.'

Suitably chastened, the next morning I rose early, trotted round the grounds and came back feeling most self-righteous. The following morning again saw me off, while not sprinting, at least at a gentle canter, only to meet others striding along on their way back! It rather took the wind out of my sails. There was me thinking I was the only one who had listened, and I was but an 'also ran'!

On the third day we were joined by our male colleagues, so that we could share what we had discovered and how we felt about ministry together. A few weeks earlier David had told me he was coming up to Wydale on the Wednesday. I wondered why he was coming and then remembered: 'Oh yes, you've been invited because you are my incumbent.' To which he replied, 'I'm not your incumbent, I'm your colleague!' It was a good day that we were able to spend together. After the main discussions and being together in groups, David and I went for a walk in the grounds, and I believe that during that time we were able to see at least some of the way ahead for us both together, to agree that we should take things as they came, and be open to one another and to where God was leading us both in our ministry.

At the end of any conference you only remember impressions, snatches of conversations, an odd phrase. So it was for me on this occasion, and the words that remain with me, and always will, were the final sentence in a talk by a wise priest, John: 'Don't expect great wonders after mid-May – not more than you have experienced so far!' I hold those words dear, as a reminder of the wonderful experiences so far, beyond expectation or telling, and of the future which I can safely leave in God's hands, knowing there will be surprises, wonders and delights, whatever happens.

Our conference finished on a high as we were joined by the person who had been such an inspiration of women to the priesthood, Dame Christian Howard. With a long and distinguished record throughout the world for her work for the Church, she has held high positions internationally as well as nationally on synods, councils and committees. With her rapier-sharp mind, a delivery of words to outshine the greatest of political orators, and a wisdom coupled with deep faith and humility, she has become one of the best known and most respected churchwomen of our time. But to us, even more than all that put together, she is our dear friend, the one who has not only showed passionate support for our ministry but love for us as individuals, her friends. We wanted to give her a gift to express our love for her, but what? All sorts of ideas flew back and forth, and in the end we decided to each contribute a piece of writing on a sheet of A4 size paper to be put in an album, representing our lives, and our love.

This proved to be the perfect gift, and Christian's face as she looked at those pages which represented so many lives in which she had played such a great part was pure happiness and delight – and for many of us the tears flowed, in thankfulness for this great lady, our dear friend.

We finished on a party note with a celebration iced cake, candles and all, for it was all our birthdays, as we prepared for our lives as priests. And who cut the cake? Who else but Christian, and the cheers and the tears were a fitting end to our week together. It had been a very special week in all our lives, and one which had brought us closer together, closer to the Lord and into a closer understanding of what lay ahead. Just two months to go – but for now there was work to do, it was time for home.

12
The Tree of Life

She and I sat together in the upstairs room at the Retreat House, facing the large window through which we could see the panoramic view over the dale to the distant hills. We talked about her life, the twenty-one years she had already lived. 'She's but a girl, what does she know about the big wide world?' I thought, forgetting of course just how much I had crammed into my first twenty-one years of life. She spoke articulately and enthusiastically about her family, home and upbringing; she knew and appreciated that she had been privileged above many others in having a Christian home, and parents who had given her the very best materially, educationally and spiritually. She had been blessed with great intellectual abilities, and the right attitude towards them, doing well at school, which had led her to Oxford University, where she was now nearing the end of her degree course. She told me of the challenges and delights of study, friendships and travel, of her hopes for the future and what had brought her to this place at this time.

Here she was at a selection conference, offering herself as a candidate for training for the priesthood. Over forty years earlier, I had sat in a similar situation; in fact I had been two years younger than her –

and miles away in background, education and experience. I had left school at fourteen, glad to be released from the drudgery of a secondary modern school, hopping from job to job, my only experience of the outside world limited to a small Cheshire town and the surrounding area. My theological education was derived only from Sunday sermons and 'Youth for Christ' evangelists proclaiming 'the good news of Jesus'. The number of books I had read on the Christian faith could have been contained on my bedside table. Yet I had been bold enough to offer myself for full-time service within the Church – and what was more amazing, had been accepted! I had now to revise my views on whether the girl beside me had experienced more or less than I had in the same position. It was just different, surely. As we talked I began to realise that two things were the same for both of us, our loving and caring upbringing by our parents, who gave us all they could, and that sure sense of calling by God to offer ourselves in service.

As I explored that sense of calling with her, what came through was of a maturity beyond her years, her close relationship with God and her openness to what he was asking of her, and her willing obedience to follow. As I talked with her and listened to her story, I delighted in her, and for her, and for the Church. Here was the promise and hope for the future, and I was being given the joy of seeing something of that potential here and now. Our formal interview over, we relaxed, and talked about other things, sharing anecdotes and common interests.

'When are you being priested?' she asked.

'May the twenty-first; won't be long now,' I said.

She looked thoughtful. 'It must have seemed a long time, the waiting. I don't think those of us coming to offer now can really realise what you have been through all these years.'

I shared with her some of my experiences along the way, especially some of the funny ones. 'It may have been hard, but it's been very good, I've enjoyed all my ministry so far and I intend to enjoy it in the future, however long or short a time that is,' I assured her.

After she left me to go off to her next interview, I sat there gazing out across the garden, over the valley to the hills beyond, and the words of the psalmist came, from Psalm 121: 'I lift up my eyes to the hills. From whence does my help come? My help comes from the Lord, who made heaven and earth' – and an overwhelming sense of thankfulness and joy swept over me. Thankfulness for the past – it had been good, so very good; and as for the future, here I was on the verge of my sixty-second birthday, looking forward to a new life as a priest beginning in just a few weeks' time. A new start at sixty-two – 'It can't be bad,' I thought. What if I had remained in industry as I had planned many years before, or taken up the challenge of a new career when the children had grown up? By now I would have been retired or redundant. Yet by following what I had sometimes found a very strange path indeed, the calling of God, here I was about to be launched into a brand new challenge, not just for me and for others like me, but for the Church and for the world. I was part of that, in at the beginning, at the ripe old age of sixty-two.

I thought of the girl who had just left me. Twenty-one! Would I like to exchange places with her, or at least be her age again? I decided, 'Definitely no!' I would not exchange the years I had lived, all the people I had known, the happenings, the varied situations, the fun and the fervour, for the gift of years. There was nothing wrong with being who I was at this time, being 'a golden oldie' – after all, gold is precious, durable and appreciated! As I gazed out of the window the sun came out, touching the scene in front of me, bringing out the colours and the contours. I could see small moving objects in the distance, vehicles travelling the far-off road, caught by the sun, like moving stars. People on the move – so small compared with the grandeur of the countryside, the hills, the sky above, and yet all part of God's wonderful world. Like those of us here at the conference, we were travellers, selectors and candidates making our way by faith on our journey, and sharing this part of the road together, lit by the light of God's presence.

I had been a selector at many such conferences before, and always delighted in being part of the process, sharing in the lives and hopes of so many, hearing the account of how they felt God had been calling them to offer themselves for the ministry. Yet I had approached this particular conference with a slight feeling of unease and trepidation, for it would be different; this time there would be women candidates for priesthood. Up until now that had not been possible, even though for some time it had seemed probable. Now, with the legislation completed, it was possible for a woman to have her vocation for the priesthood tested, and here were my first candidates. I knew the chairman of the selection conference; he was one of the bishops who would not be ordaining women. What would it be like working with him at this conference? How would he deal with this new situation? What about the other candidates? No doubt they would hold varying views, so how would they gel together as a conference, enabling each one to give a true picture of themselves?

My fears and unease were quickly dispelled. The bishop – wise, godly and experienced – set the scene, not avoiding the issues, but with such loving and caring openness and directness that we were all at ease with one another. We knew that what was being prayed for and worked for, was to know God's will for each one there. At the end of the conference, as we all met for the last time together, there was a sense of belonging, understanding and caring each for each. Any barriers had been broken down, we had all been able to be ourselves, and to trust the Lord for and with each other. It was also my birthday, and the cook had made a giant birthday cake for me, which we all shared with that last cup of tea before the candidates departed for home, and we the selectors got on with our reports and discussions on them. As I blew out the candles and dug the knife into the cake before it was divided up between us all, I thought of the Holy Communion service we'd all just shared in, the words 'Though we are many, we are one body, because we all share in one bread', and here we were sharing in a birthday cake as well, as any family would, before going our separate ways. It was a relaxing fun end to the time we had all shared together.

Later that evening, with our reports completed and before we settled down to discuss them, we selectors had dinner together. As it was my birthday I made sure we had a bottle of wine to share with our meal too. I raised my glass. 'To the Church of England,' I said. 'God bless her and all who serve in her!' – and under my breath added, 'Thank you, Lord, that I'm part of it!'

Only a few weeks later I was again heading towards the same Retreat House, this time battling with the Bank Holiday Monday crowds who were going to the coast for the day. I realised I should have given myself more time to get there, but I had misguidedly thought all the traffic would have gone before I set out – not so, we were all jammed together, and I was getting rather hot and bothered. To be late for the retreat – it really wasn't on. As I staggered into the house I found I was not the only late-comer, in fact most people had been held up, and I was not the last to arrive. The staff greeted us warmly, showing us to our rooms, and then reminded us that lunch was ready for us in the dining room. 'But don't rush, take your time, no hurry.' Words that were to be the emphasis of that retreat, and very welcome words too.

We had been given the afternoon to unwind, to catch up on news, to do whatever we wanted to do before beginning the retreat proper, and going into silence. Four of us decided to go for a walk and call in at a craft centre not far down the road. 'It would be nice to buy something to remind us of this week,' one person said, and so we all decided that was a good idea – until we saw the prices! Everything was of the highest standards – beautiful pictures, exquisite materials, dainty china – but so expensive. I settled for a bright red tin mug in the 'reduced' section, but hardly a suitable memento of such an occasion! One of our number had a bright idea: 'I think I'll get a plant or shrub, they are not very expensive and will last for ages.' We viewed the plant section outside and decided this was a bit nearer our price range. So we settled on plants. I bought a lavender, small and neat, and with a hint, the tiniest hint of fragrance to come. 'Sort of symbolic,' I thought to myself.

My purchase completed I took another look at the postcards and assorted cards on sale. One took my eye. It showed a hedgehog driving a bright red car, and looking very cheerful indeed, with a big smile on his face, for he was throwing away his 'L' plate. The card read, 'Liberated, legal, licensed . . . and lethal. Congratulations!' 'Hey look at this!' I shouted to my friends. 'It rather describes us doesn't it?' I am sure the proprietor of the shop must have thought us quite mad as we all bought the same card. Surely we couldn't all have known someone who had just passed their driving test! I bought two of them. One I sent to one of our number who could not come on the retreat. She was a sister of the Order of the Holy Paraclete, Sister Marion Eva, a fellow deacon and also to be ordained priest, but she had fallen and broken her leg, and so was unable to be with us. She is a great character, a wonderful friend to us all, and we were all thinking of her and praying for her; as we knew she would be for us. I decided the card was just right for her; after all, she would be on wheels to be ordained, in a wheelchair, and so I ear-marked one card for her.

The other one? I decided that was from me to me! Yes, I had been liberated, I was about to be legal – ordained a priest – and I was already licensed as a minister. As for the lethal bit – well, I have to admit I am pretty lethal at times, not least when driving my red car! As for 'congratulations', why not? It was a lively start to our retreat, the conversation and chatter was fun, but the best was to come, when silence descended. That was bliss. The quietness slowed us all down, we could taste our food, smell the flowers, observe creation and worship God unhurried, undisturbed by any demands.

The letter from Bishopthorpe Palace telling us about the ordination retreat had said, 'The Archbishop's intention, as with every Ordination Retreat is that this occasion should be a cherished space for you to fix your thoughts and prayers on what lies ahead, released from the ties, duties, chores and distractions that normally surround you . . .' So it was to prove for us. Our chaplain, Andrew Girling, a wise and experienced parish priest, who is also a hospice chaplain, cared for us warmly and prayerfully, being always available, and yet never intruding. The retreat, led by Sister Janet of the Order of the Holy Paraclete, was based on the passage in the first book of Kings when the Queen of Sheba came to meet King Solomon, and on the Song of Mary, the Magnificat – and we were guided to think about the gifts we had been given, the gifts we brought with us now to share in our new ministry as priests. To be able to do this, to have time to reflect, without being forced to do anything but just 'be' was something very precious indeed for all of us.

On our last day we were given a drawing of a tree, with its roots, trunk, leaves, buds and fruits. We were asked to try and see this tree as our life, all the different parts of it from our beginning, and to make it our Tree of Life, a personal thanksgiving for all we had received. We were encouraged to write down our thanksgivings for where we had come from; the influences on our life; the structure of our life today; our family, friends and church; everything we enjoyed, our achievements and our hopes;

and to thank God that he had brought us to this stage in our lives; and then to offer this tree of our life to God as we came to the final Holy Communion service together at the end of the retreat.

It would be difficult to set apart any one thing during the retreat that had the deepest influence on me, for it all was so right; it was, I believe, a foretaste not just of the earthly journey ahead but of heaven itself. But that time spent thinking and praying about my 'Tree of Life' brought everything into a deeper focus, and a greater sense of God's loving purpose in my life. Sister Janet's words, 'You are pioneers, this is awesome, go forward in joy; we don't know what the future holds, but God does,' have come back to me over and over again, and I know will continue to do so.

I sat in the garden with my 'Tree of Life' in my hand, and looked at an old tree, or what remained of it, beside me. It was a beautiful stately old copper beech, a very special tree, but it had been terribly damaged in a great storm, and much to the sadness of everyone it was feared it might have to be demolished. But a sculptor named Colin Wilburn saw that tree, the trunk still sturdy, though broken, and he had a vision for it. He turned it into a living sculpture of Jacob's Ladder, reaching up from earth to heaven, the steps leading up the tree, into the space at the top. Something that had been so great and beautiful was broken, deformed then transformed, to continue to inspire all who came to that place.

When I finished writing up my 'Tree of Life', I went and placed my hand on the living tree. It felt warm, comforting and strong, the ladder so inviting, I almost wanted to climb up to see where it went – but knew my limits, tree climbing is not one of my accomplishments! But I did not need to climb it, only to look and wonder and thank God for yet another gift to me in this living parable in front of me, which I could see and handle, and almost become part of. I thanked him too for the vision and skill of the sculptor, doing his part, sharing his gifts so people like me could gain encouragement and fresh vision for their lives too. I patted the tree goodbye. 'See you again, I expect,' I said, and then went into the chapel with my 'Tree of Life', my glad offering to the Lord before taking with him the next step into the future.

13
What's in a Name?

I had obviously caused a
bit of a problem. I could tell that by the way Joan
hesitantly approached me while I was sorting out
some books at the back of the church before the
morning service. 'Margaret, can I ask you something? I hope you don't mind me asking but . . .'
She seemed very anxious and nervous, not at all her
usual self.

'What's the matter?' I asked. It was evident there
was something bothering her.

'I've been wondering . . . well, some of us have
been wondering . . . What do we call you after you
are ordained priest?'

I smiled at her. 'What do you call me now?'

She looked doubtful. 'We call you Margaret,
but . . .'

'So then you call me Margaret afterwards too. I'll
still be the same person won't I?'

She still looked rather uncertain, not at all convinced. I tried to explain that there were those, like
her, who know me well, who called me Margaret,
always had done, and that would not change. There
were one or two who liked the more formal ap-
proach, who called me Mrs Cundiff – and I would
still be Mrs Cundiff. 'After all,' I said, 'you call the
vicar David or Mr Woollard, it's just the same.'

She hesitated. 'Well, yes, but I still think it's different . . .'

Michael, our treasurer, raised the same subject, in a slightly different way later that day when we were talking outside the church gate. 'What are you going to be called, then, after your ordination? You were the deaconess before you were the parish deacon, now you are going to be a priest but you won't be the parish priest, so what will you be?'

I thought about that one. 'I'm described as "assistant curate" on the list that has been issued by Bishopthorpe, so that's what I am.' I saw no problem about that, after all, it simply meant 'assistant in the cure of souls' – in modern words 'assistant in the ministry'. I was quite happy to be called that, working alongside the vicar. Titles have never concerned me.

But the vicar himself raised the matter again that week so I reminded him of the official title 'assistant curate'. He shook his head. 'I can't put you down in the parish magazine as that. It sounds so junior, it doesn't describe what you are. No, not assistant curate.'

'How about "associate minister" then?' I suggested.

He didn't seem to think that was the right description either. 'I'll think of something, there must be some way of making clear what your position is.'

So we left the discussion. After all, there were far more important things to think about than ecclesiastical titles.

At a meeting in York later that week I found myself sitting next to the Archdeacon of York, George Austin, a well-known opponent of women priests, but a very good friend of mine all the same.

When he first came to the diocese there were many who thought we would not get on, holding totally opposite views, but get on we did and do. We are both involved in radio work, and respect one another as seasoned broadcasters. We both have the same sense of humour, and we agree on most subjects, apart from women priests, on which we agree to differ. George put an arm round me and announced, 'I know what I'm going to call you after you are ordained – Mother Margaret!'

'Don't you dare, or I will call you Father George,' I threatened – with a smile, of course!

Since then I have been told of one parish who are used to calling their priests Father, who now call their woman priest Father Helen – but somehow it doesn't seem to hit the right note! No doubt in time the Church will come up with some official form of address, although for myself I am happy to be addressed variously as the Reverend Margaret Cundiff, Margaret, Mrs Cundiff, or 'our curate' – after all, what's in a name?

The subject came up again a week or so later, but this time a suggestion was made tongue in cheek, to tease me, to bring me down to earth. I had decided to send out cards to friends, announcing my forthcoming ordination and asking them to pray for me. I had studied the wording on various such cards before deciding on my own. Eventually I chose a simple white card with the words, 'Please pray for Margaret Joan Cundiff to be ordained Priest in York Minster on Saturday, 21st May 1994 at 11.00 am. "The Eve of Pentecost".' I added two lines of a hymn at the bottom: 'We'll praise him for all that is past, and trust him for all that's to come', and my address and telephone number. When I received the cards back from the printers they looked so formal and stark, that I went out and bought packets of brightly coloured butterflies, candles and stars and stuck them on the cards to make them look more cheerful. Since such an occasion was surely about new life, light and guidance, why not show it in a visual way?

Meeting the former Archdeacon, Leslie Stanbridge, in York, I gave him one of my cards. He looked at it very intently, and then beamed at me. 'Yes, it does suit you, that's what I shall call you,' he pronounced firmly. I wasn't sure what he was getting at, there was no form of address on the card, only my name, Margaret Joan Cundiff. 'Eve,' he said. 'Yes, that's what I shall call you, Eve.' Why on earth did he want to call me Eve, I wondered, and demanded an explanation. He grinned at me, the grin I knew so well, the one he reserved for occasions when he knew he had got the better of someone. 'Look, then, it says it here.' He underlined with his finger the words 'The Eve of Pentecost'. 'Very suitable indeed, from now on that's what I shall call you, Eve of Pentecost', and chuckling to himself he made off towards the Minster. 'Point to you, Leslie,' I said under my breath. Ah well, there were worse names I could be called, though somehow I didn't think Eve was quite me. A former broadcasting colleague and Methodist minister wrote, 'We knew you'd do it in the end. Where would you like to be Bishop of? Margaret Mablethorpe has a certain ring!' and another addressed the envelope to me 'The Reverend Margaret Cundiff, BBC, VIP, HGV'. BBC yes; VIP – to those who love me, thank goodness I am a VIP; but HGV? I know I drive my car like a tank sometimes but I doubt whether I would get a Heavy Goods Vehicle licence on the strength of that!

As the time drew nearer towards the ordination day, more and more post arrived, from all parts of the world. I was completely amazed by it all. There were letters, cards and gifts, many from people I hardly knew, some I didn't know at all, who had heard me on the radio, or read one of my books or been at a meeting I had taken. I began to realise what a lot of love and prayer was surrounding me – and all the other candidates as well, for they too were having the same joyful experience.

Some of the most moving letters were from those who were not in favour of the ordination of women to the priesthood, who found it hard to accept, and yet wrote to assure me of their prayers and love for me as a person. As one priest wrote, 'I know this is a time of joy for you all, but it is a period of stress for me. I trust it will not spoil my friendship with those women deacons whom I find it hard to accept as priests. In spite of that, please be assured of my prayers . . .' Another wrote, 'I am a supporter of women's ordination NOW but I did need to be convinced as to why the Church should change after so many centuries. The strident lobby worried me, who I suspected as being Moles for the Womens Lib Movement – you changed all that . . .' Yet another dear friend, an elderly priest who had been so much part of my spiritual journey, wrote lovingly:

As you probably know I have had great difficulties in accepting the Ordination of Women . . . However, as the Church of England approached the matter in prayer to the Holy Spirit for guidance I have accepted the decision made by Synod. I must admit I am not finding it easy to adjust to the decision, so I know you will pray for us both, bless you. It does not prevent me from saying a warm welcome to you, Margaret, in becoming a priest in our lovely Church of England . . . the Church of England is in the wonderful position of being both Catholic and Reformed . . . God bless you richly . . .

So many letters, and it would be impossible to say which one meant most. They were all equally special, from the funny and jokey to those which almost preached a sermon to me. Some sent poems and verses, or wrote pages and pages, others simply put 'God bless you'. Yet maybe the one which remains most with me, and will always do so, was the last letter I ever received from the former Archbishop of York, Stuart Blanch. As his Broadcasting Officer I had worked for him during his years at York, and what years they were. I learned so much from him. He enlarged my vision of the Church, inspired me to dig deeper into scripture and theological study, encouraged me to write and supported me through personal difficulties. He was a great archbishop, with a boyish sense of fun, and a good, wise friend – they were very special years.

Our friendship continued after his retirement, and his letters were always a delight, always encouraging me to 'go for it'. He had written earlier in the year saying how pleased he was that the way was now open for women priests. '. . . I think the ordination of women has come at just the right time, adding a new dimension and maybe a new appeal to the outsider's view of the Church, so praise the Lord!' When I was able to write and tell him the date was fixed he wrote back immediately: 'May 21st will I am sure mean a lot to you and crown a long process by which you have grown in the faith yourself and excelled in making it available to others. So every blessing for the day and for whatever 1994 holds for you. As ever. Stuart.'

As I cheerfully posted a card to him with the message, 'Will let you know how it all goes,' little did I realise that his time on this earth was rapidly drawing to a close, and that a few days after my ordination he would be laid to rest in a country churchyard in Oxfordshire. '. . . whatever 1994 holds . . .' he had written. None of us knows what a day holds, leave alone a year. Stuart Blanch's death brought me up sharp, a reminder that 'in the midst of life we are in death'. As I began my new life as a priest, he began his new life in heaven. There would be no more letters from him to cheer and inspire me, but there was the knowledge that in that vast 'communion of saints' he would be part of that great throng which always surrounds us, 'the Church on earth and in heaven'.

For me, approaching week beginning May 21st, there was not a cloud in the sky. I knew, I thought, exactly what would happen. I had planned the final 'count down' of days with military-like precision. Nothing could go wrong at this stage – or could it?

14
Best Foot Forward

As I stumped up the paths on a hot Monday morning my halo was getting tighter and tighter. I was delivering my Christian Aid envelopes, showing those who said they had 'no time this week'. No time indeed! If I had time, so had everybody else. Here I was, getting ready to be ordained a priest on Saturday, but still taking my full share in the work of Christian Aid Week. Whether it was the halo, or my being lost in thought, suddenly a pain shot through my right foot. I had trodden on an iron bar which lay across the path. I rubbed my ankle, shook it, put my foot gingerly to the ground and limped on. By now the halo had well and truly slipped, and I was glad when all the envelopes were delivered.

Later that evening Peter remarked, 'Michael said he saw you this morning and you were limping.'

'No', I said, 'I don't think so.' – subject closed.

The next day the ankle was really hurting. I was limping but, trying to believe in mind over matter, went on. It was in the middle of the night that I was forced to admit all was not well. I began to cry to myself; the rehearsal for the ordination was the next evening, how would I be able to walk round the Minster?

Peter heard me crying and said quietly, 'What's the matter, love?'

I sniffled, 'I'm not going to make it on Saturday, I know I'm not.'

An arm came round me. 'Of course you are, you know that. It's right for you . . .'

I sniffled louder. 'I've no worries about being ordained, it's my foot.'

So the sorry tale came out, and I decided I had better seek some advice from my friendly pharmacist.

'It's like this,' I told them in the chemist's shop next morning, 'I've got to get round the Minster tonight. I need a strapping, some pain killers and can I have some of that stuff footballers use?' (I had seen miracles performed on football pitches by trainers with cans, surely it would work for me.) All my requirements were produced, and I set to work.

As I squirted the can vigorously, Peter said, 'I think you are going into Operation Overkill with that.'

I didn't care, all I needed was a foot that would take me round with the other. It did ease, well enough to get round. It was strange being in the Minster with so few people around that evening. Instead of the thronging crowds, there were just those of us who were to be ordained, the Bishop of Selby, his chaplain, the Archdeacon of Cleveland who was to preach, and those who would be in charge of arrangements. The Bishop, who would be ordaining us, explained about the rehearsal.

'It's like this,' he said. 'When you learn to dance you have to watch your feet, so you can enjoy the dance. Tonight we watch our feet, so on Saturday we can dance!'

Thinking about my feet, I sincerely hoped so! As the rehearsal went on we all relaxed. There was a sense of 'in-it-togetherness', of love and friendship, and the Bishop, by his manner, his care and his encouragement to each one of us, made that evening very special.

At the end of the rehearsal he said, 'Well, that's fine, but let me say this. Whatever you do on Saturday, it will be right. I want you to be carefree on Saturday, so don't worry about it, and remember, whatever you do, do it with assurance and dignity.'

I thought I might manage the first, but I was not sure about the second! As I drove home that evening I felt relaxed. Sure enough, my foot hurt, but I knew I would make it; God had not brought me this far to trip me up on the last day. Anyway, maybe it was good for me to be brought down from my self-righteousness about delivering those envelopes and given something else to think about.

The next two days flew by like a dream, getting ready for visitors, answering the telephone and reading all the messages of goodwill, the letters and cards, besides trying to make some time to be quiet. I was beginning to feel overtaken by events, and I so much wanted to have space; and there was – amazingly so. Gaps appeared in my timetable and I took them, and enjoyed them, allowing God's peace to wash over me, to enfold me. So it was with a quiet mind and a ready heart that I awoke to the new day of Saturday, May 21st, the Eve of Pentecost. Here it was, at last.

The day dawned like anything but a May day, more like October, dull and cold, with the threat of rain.

'Please let it keep dry until everyone gets there,' I prayed. After all, I thought, the God who could stay the waters of the Red Sea could surely keep back the rain today! At least we all got into the Minster before the rain came down, and for that I, and several thousand other people, were truly grateful.

How different the Minster looked, felt and sounded from the quiet evening of the rehearsal. Now there was an air of celebration, excitement and activity. Arriving early, I was able to see my family settled in their reserved seats with a good view, and then go in search of various friends in the vast congregation. People were pouring in, the seats rapidly being filled, and I was so glad I had advised my friends to come early.

The Minster had the air of a wedding, and rightly so. It was to be a time when we would give ourselves freely and joyfully to the service of our Lord and his Church, and be united for all time, legally, with love!

I saw coming towards me my former vicar, David Bond. He was almost bouncing along, his face alight with happiness, and hugging me he exclaimed, 'It's here at last, love. I am so happy!' Then together we went to greet folk from the parish. For David and Dorothy it was a very poignant time, not just being there in the Minster for the ordination, but because it was the first time since leaving St James' and Wistow the previous summer that they had met their Selby friends again. Now David was their 'former vicar', but friendship is always the same. There is no need for titles when you are friends, and reunions with those you love are very special.

It is customary for Anglican priests present and robed at an ordination to assist the Bishop with the

105

laying on of hands, but in our case, with twenty-two candidates, it was likely to be an almost impossible task. So we had been asked to have only two nominees each. I had no hesitation in the choice of mine, the two Davids – my present vicar, David Woollard, the one with whom I would set out on my priestly ministry, and David Bond, who had shared with me the thirteen years leading up to this time. He had shared in my anxieties and excitement, my fears, frustrations and delights. He had prayed for, and cared for, and supported me, and still did, and I wanted him to be right there when the moment for ordination came. After all, he was so much part of it already, the moment was his to share, to lay hands on me as he had done so many times in the past as we shared in the healing ministry together, just as there were so many times when I had laid hands on him, praying for God's grace and support, wisdom and power in his ministry. So this was a culmination of so much, and he would be there beside me.

David Woollard was delighted when I asked him to be a nominee, but said, 'I would love to, but you have so many friends. I have only just come. I don't want to take the place of someone who is special to you, just because I'm here now.' He looked anxiously at me.

'David,' I said, 'I've asked you because I want you. Maybe we have only known each other a short time, but I have no doubt that I want you beside me at that moment of ordination.'

The two Davids! Together we would be part of history, together make a new start in our lives and ministry, and I thanked God for their willingness to share with me in that unique and precious moment of my life.

As the time drew near for the service to begin, I went to robe with the other candidates in the Lady Chapel. By now the air of excitement and busyness had changed to a quiet, almost subdued hush. We were together and yet in those few minutes were detaching ourselves from one another. We each had our own thoughts, memories, hopes, and maybe fears. I did what probably all the others were doing, offered myself afresh to the Lord in penitence, knowing my own unworthiness, yet in joy, knowing that he accepted me as me, and asking for his presence to fill us all afresh with his Holy Spirit. As the great procession began to move into the main body of the Minster, I was filled with a great surge of joy. It really was happening, and to me, the day I had longed for all these years had come!

So into the welcome of the crowded Minster, conscious of the support of our families, friends, fellow clergy and ministers, and with an overwhelming sense of the presence of the Lord, we joined together as one, and the ordination service began. When the candidates, all twenty-two of us, moved into the sanctuary, our names were read out by the Archdeacon of Cleveland, with the places where we were to serve as priests, and the work we were to be engaged in. As I stood there listening to the familiar names of friends, I praised God for each one of them. We had come a long way together to this day, now it was 'one more step' – a giant leap for us. To hear the words 'Margaret Joan Cundiff, to serve as Assistant Curate of St James', Selby, and Broadcasting Officer' I could almost hear my old friend Derek Jameson, saying one of his famous lines, 'Does he mean us?' Then came the moment, the solemn and awesome moment, when the Bishop of Selby addressed the congregation:

'Is it therefore your will that they should be ordained priest?'

We faced the congregation. What would happen? Would anyone say 'No'? Would there be any demonstration, rejection? Without hesitation a resounding roar went up from the thousands gathered there, 'It is!' The tension dropped, I felt the colour return to my cheeks, and took a deep breath as I heard the Bishop say:

'Will you uphold them in their ministry?'

The answer came again, loud and clear: 'We will!'

So came the time of ordination as each one of us went and knelt before the Bishop, to receive the laying on of hands, and to hear those words:

'Send down the Holy Spirit upon your servant for the office and work of a priest in your Church.'

I felt many hands laid upon me. I knew there would be those of the Bishop, the two Davids and who else I did not know. But what I did know was the hand of the Lord, welcoming and empowering me for the new life ahead.

Later, each of us was presented with a Bible with the words: 'Receive this Book, as a sign of the authority which God has given you this day to preach the gospel of Christ, and to minister his Holy Sacraments.'

Then the sharing of the Peace, with so many rushing forward with love to greet us. Sharing that love with my family. Kneeling with them to receive the sacrament of Holy Communion together. There we were, my father, my husband Peter, our children Julian and Alison, 'our family' and also part of the great family of God in that place, and on earth and in heaven. Heaven was all around us at that moment, heaven was here and now!

The hymns during the service had been well-known and traditional. We had been asked to submit a list of our choice – and I suppose it was rather like the 'top ten', but in this case the top five. The hymn after the Communion, though, might have been less well known, and I had not included it in my particular list of favourites. But how right it was! The tune was lively and swinging, the words said just what needed to be heard by us. The first verse was a series of questions, Jesus saying:

> Will you come and follow me if I but call your name.
> Will you go where you don't know and never be the same?
> Will you let my love be shown,
> Will you let my name be known,
> Will you let my life be grown in you and you in me?

And the last verse, which in that mighty throng I was able to make my own personal response:

> Lord, your summons echoes true when you but call my name.
> Let me turn and follow you and never be the same.
> In your company I'll go
> Where your love and footsteps show,
> Thus I'll move and live and grow in you and you in me.

Called, known, accepted! Some words from the prophet Isaiah, which have been so special to me in my life, came again into my mind and heart: 'Fear not, for I have redeemed you; I have called you by name, you are mine.'

We knelt for the Bishop's blessing, and to his words of dismissal, 'Go in peace, to love and serve the Lord', we joyfully replied, 'In the name of Christ. Amen.'

The procession began to make its way back through the Minster. I was glad we were not singing a hymn, I felt too full for words. Then as we, the newly ordained priests, began to move, the congregation rose as one in applause. It grew louder and louder, faces smiling in welcome, hands clapping like thunder. I am sure we floated back. Then there was the official presentation of documents, the legal papers, the photographs, and we were led out on to the steps to the waiting and welcoming crowd.

As we all separated, I rejoined my family.

'You looked ever so pale when you came in, Mum,' confided Alison. 'When you went up to be ordained Julian had his head down and was muttering, "Don't slip mother, don't slip!" Then when he saw you were all right he said, "Well done, Mum, well done."'

She squeezed my hand. 'Well done, Mum, you did it beautifully.'

Someone else said, 'I was amazed, you just knelt down so confidently and gracefully.'

Beautifully, confidently, and gracefully – not my natural graces, but I had been held safe and secure in God's hand at that moment, as I had been all my life, and always would be. Now a new life was beginning. But first, on to the party!

15
A Priest Forever

The rain, which had been a sullen drizzle since mid-morning, now came down with a vengeance. We drove back to Selby in a downpour, but nothing could dampen our joy and exhilaration. Jumping over the puddles in our dash from the car park to the church hall, we entered a festival of colour and light. The hall had been decorated with balloons, flowers and streamers. The tables were laid as for a wedding buffet, and on the far wall an enormous mural showed a lady in cassock, surplice and stole leaping through a field of flowers, holding aloft a red umbrella, with the words 'Feed My Sheep' while a bemused sheep grazed beside her. In her other hand she held a red case on which were the words 'DIY Home Communion Kit'. At the bottom of the mural the reference Proverbs 31. 30–31 ('Charm is deceitful, and beauty is vain, but a woman who fears the Lord is to be praised. Give her of the fruit of her hands, and let her works praise her in the gates.'). It had been designed and painted by the Mackwell family who are all very artistic, and added great fun to the day. Some of our church members had been working hard all day to prepare for the party, and had given up the chance of going to the ordination service so they could make sure all was ready for when we arrived back. Their love and unselfishness brought tears to my eyes. They had done all this to make my day, and I was so conscious of how many times I had failed to care for them as I should. I had put other things before them, and yet they were so supportive of me. It was a reminder yet again that ministry is a two-way thing; giving and receiving are both vital ingredients. Everything in that hall spoke of a labour of love – the hard work of preparation, the food, the drink, the decorations, and of course the people. People from my past, my present, and hopefully my future. Family and friends. Not only members of our two parishes but people from the wider Christian community in Selby, former vicars and their wives, deanery clergy – so many beaming faces and outstretched hands, welcoming me home as a priest. A priest, yes – but still Margaret, their Margaret.

The centre-piece of the buffet was a most beautifully iced and decorated cake, with the words 'Congratulations, Margaret'. It held a special significance, for it had been made and decorated by Fiona and her mother June. I had known them since Fiona was a little girl. The family was very much involved with the church, and in a few weeks time I would be conducting the marriage service of Fiona and her husband-to-be, Ian. Fiona was thrilled that it would be my first wedding as a priest, so here was my cake. It was exactly the same as her wedding cake, and marked a sharing of our lives, of the events of love that bound us together. When it came to the cutting of the cake I shared it with the one who had cut a wedding cake with me many years before, my husband Peter. Thirty-four years ago we had set out on our adventure of marriage which had been filled to the brim with experiences of all kinds, not least producing two children, now grown to maturity. Here we were cutting the cake which marked a new beginning in the wider community, and still together in it.

The occasion was also tinged with sadness, for the party was a joint one to also say goodbye to our Reader, Colin. Colin had come to St James' eighteen years previously. A member of the Brethren, he had found it strange at first in this Anglican church, especially with a woman minister around. As he confessed later, he almost walked out the first time I preached, but then found I was 'quite sound' in what I said, and decided St James' was the place for him. As he became more and more involved in the life of the church he realised God was calling him to the ministry of Reader. It was a big step from the Brethren to being part of the Church of England establishment, wearing robes, using set forms of worship, being part of a formal structure. Yet it was right for him, and we delighted in him and for him. Colin is an outstanding preacher and teacher, counsellor and pastor to many, especially young people. We had hoped he would be with us for ever. But of course, apart from heaven there is no such thing as for ever. He had to leave us to take up new work in London. He had for a year commuted some weekends but found this was unrealistic, and so reluctantly now was making his break with us officially.

So this was the day when we formally said thank-you and goodbye to Colin, and it was Colin who made the speech at the party, welcoming me as priest. Who says God has no sense of humour! Colin also has a great sense of humour, and his speech captured the eighteen years very accurately but with a good turn of phrase. He spoke of events which had happened over the years, the things we had shared. His closing comment was: 'It's not easy to be angry with Margaret because she's so cheerful about everything, even when it's wrong! She reminds me of Pilgrim marching on with great enthusiasm, dragging the rest of us behind her . . . Margaret always manages to be unfailingly cheerful!'

Yes, I suppose Colin was right. I do want to 'drag them kicking and screaming into the kingdom of heaven', and I do what a radio producer advised me to do, many years ago, 'smile when you kick 'em'. Unfailingly cheerful though? Not always. I do have my moments, but it is in those moments of gloom and despair and frustration with myself, the Church, the world, when I want to say, 'Enough, I've had it', that the Lord picks me up, dusts me down, sets me on my feet and moves me on. He gives me all I need, and more. As he shows me myself, what can I do but smile? After all, if God can love and use someone like me, he can do anything with anyone, and I want to be right there to see him do it, too!

I found the party quite overwhelming. Like the ordination service itself, it was filled with the power of love, human and divine, mixed together in a heady cocktail of celebration. Perhaps the crowning moment was when the vicar presented me with the gift which had been contributed to by members of both parishes, St James' and All Saints' Wistow, my family and friends – a Home Communion set. Beautifully designed in silver and gold, it contained everything I would need to take Holy Communion, each piece sparkling, set in a leather case.

As David held it out to me he said, 'I can't think of a more fitting and more glorious present.'

As I took it and looked at it and knew what it represented I was almost lost for words, for never in my wildest dreams had I really imagined that one day I would have placed into my hands such a gift, and the authority to use it. How could I express my thanks? Words were inadequate, but I knew that the only real thank-you would be by using it, sharing it. For after all it was not just a gift to me, but one that belonged to all of us.

Sleep did not come easily that night. It was hard to wind down and relax. I slept fitfully, and found myself wide awake in the middle of the night. It was dark and quiet, with not a sound, too early even for the dawn chorus. I relived in my mind some of the moments of the day before, and then the panic set in. Today I would begin my priestly ministry. I would celebrate for the first time as a priest. I was tired. I was not ready. I wanted time. It had all been too much at once. I wanted to get away on my own, to get everything settled and sorted, to come to terms with all the emotion of yesterday. That 'pre-wedding, pre-birth, pre-ordination' feeling had hit me hard. 'Even a day would do it,' I thought. Just one day away on my own, and then I could begin, then I could cope. Attractive as such a prospect was, it was impossible, and I knew it. So I uttered a prayer I keep for such occasions, a one-word prayer: 'Help!' I cannot remember receiving an answer, because I fell asleep, and when I woke up the sun was shining, the birds were on their second round of song, and a mug of coffee was beside the bed. God has many ways of answering prayer.

When we arrived at church I could sense the excitement. The hangings of brilliant red to mark the feast of Pentecost, the bright displays of flowers, and the churchwardens standing with their polished wands of office, all made it look quite dazzling. David had decided we would have a procession, and so we gathered in the vestry, the wardens, David, Colin and myself. We prayed and then stood in silence, before together joining the congregation for the opening hymn.

David was going to act as my deacon, Colin to take the prayers, my former theological college tutor and great friend Jock to read the epistle, and Peter the gospel. David had asked if I would like anyone special to preach. 'You will preach,' I told him firmly. 'Sunday is family, us. You are the vicar, and I want you to preach.'

It was a most memorable sermon. Where could we have found such a preacher? David reminded us of what had gone before, and then came to today.

Today we are witnesses of a turning-point in history. It can only happen once for the first time. The Church of England has ratified what God had long ago ordained, and today we celebrate . . . it is a marvellous, brilliant piece of God's timing that this should happen as we celebrate the great turning-point in the life of the Church, Pentecost . . .

He went on to describe that first Day of Pentecost, what it meant, the outpouring of the Holy Spirit, how the Spirit that is poured out on all believers, the Holy Spirit, was with us now. As I took my place for the first time as celebrant, flanked by David and Colin, looking out at all those gathered with us, the sense of God's Holy Spirit was so powerful, filling that place, filling me, giving me a lightness of spirit, a sense of freedom and joy, a release from the tensions, anxieties and tiredness. I was also released from myself, and enabled to be used, I believe, as God wanted, not as I had either hoped or planned, but as he did. A day to remember – yes it was. But much of it was too special to hold, to remember, to record. What happened was indescribable; words could not capture the feelings, and neither should they. That time belonged to God, and was for me at that moment. I could not hoard it, parcel it up and take it home, keep it as a memento, even hand it down. It was given, taken, consumed. It was a foretaste of heaven, the Lord's seal. Now I was to go on from that moment, that day.

Later that day I was the celebrant again. Not as in the great splendour of the morning, but with a small group in our side chapel for the evening Holy Communion service. David had been anxious about it. He had another service to go to, and was concerned about leaving me on my own.

'I wanted to be with you all day,' he said. 'I don't like leaving you on your own this evening. Will you be all right?' He looked anxious.

I laughed. 'I'm a big girl, I think I can manage all right.'

As I began that evening celebration, I suddenly realised that for the first time I was on my own. I was the priest. In the morning, although I had been the celebrant, David had been there, another priest had been present. The reality of being a priest had not quite dawned one-hundred-per-cent. That evening it did – the process was complete. What was it David had said about God's sense of timing? Truly it was marvellous and brilliant!

The words on one of the cards I had received at my ordination came into my mind: 'A Priest Forever'. In that quiet evening service I knew in my heart, in my bones, in my mind, in every part of my being, the reality of those words: 'a priest forever'. The process of becoming had happened, now it was a life of being.

'Today is the first day of the rest of your life' is a much-quoted saying. For me as a priest it was joyfully a reality. But then each day for all of us is 'the first day of the rest of your life', whoever we are, whatever we are doing, whatever comes. It is a gift to be used, in co-operation with, and loving surrender to, the giver.

I slept well that night. No fears, no panic, no regrets. Tomorrow was another day, and God was there already. I could sleep. Tomorrow – well, all would be revealed in his good time, and that was more than good enough for me!

Where Do You
Go from Here?

The more I thought about it, the more apprehensive I felt. The significance of what was about to happen was quite overwhelming, and for me it was rather frightening. What would people say, think or even do? Would anyone walk out? I had no way of knowing until it happened.

I always enjoyed being 'chaplain on duty' at York Minster, and had been delighted to be asked to join the team of clergy who gave a day every month or so as honorary chaplains. Our job was to 'loiter with intent', as it had been described, in the Minster, to be available as a 'listening ear' for anyone who wanted to talk or pray, and also to lead the brief prayers on the hour several times during the day. I remembered my first time on duty early in 1993. I had gone round and introduced myself with a cheery 'Good morning, I'm your chaplain on duty,' and had received a warm welcome, except from one lady who raised her eyebrows and said rather frostily:

'I didn't know we had *women* chaplains.'

With an air of confidence I had replied, 'Oh yes.'

She stared at me, unconvinced. 'How long have we had them?'

I looked at my watch, 'About ten minutes' – and fled!

On another occasion, when I was trying to be very official in my cassock and clerical collar, a lady stood staring hard at me.

'Can I help you?' I enquired.

'It is Mrs Cundiff isn't it?' she queried.

I assured her it was. She looked relieved.

'Oh. Only I usually see you in Safeways!'

What I often find after I have led the prayers is that people come up and shyly begin to talk and ask questions, particularly about prayer. Often they ask for prayer for themselves or for someone dear to them, and it is a privilege to be able to share just for a few minutes in their lives, and help them on their journey of faith.

So why was I feeling worried? Today had a very special difference. Up to now, as a deacon I had not been able to be the celebrant at the mid-day service of Holy Communion; a priest would come in. Today as a priest I would celebrate. I had been thrilled when a phone call from the Minster had assured me that they wanted me to celebrate, and pointed out that I would be making history as the first woman to do so. A few weeks ago it had seemed an exciting prospect, now it was rather daunting.

Peter said, 'I'll come with you, I'd like to be there.'

So together we went to the Minster. All had been prepared for me by the friendly verger but what was more, Leslie Stanbridge had come along to be with me, to assist. He put me at ease at once with his usual graciousness, and I felt safe, knowing he was right beside me. On the list of those to be prayed for was the name 'Stuart Blanch, critically ill'.

I turned to Leslie. 'Is he very ill?' I had not realised how grave the situation was.

He nodded sadly. 'I'm afraid so, Margaret. He is in the hospice now. He hasn't long.'

I felt the tears coming, and then had to pull myself together firmly.

Later, at the altar, I prayed for him and thanked God for his faithfulness, and for all the encouragement and hope he had brought to so many, praying that he might know at that moment our support for him.

I did falter once or twice, and I did, as I confessed to Leslie afterwards, use the wrong collect.

He smiled at me and said, 'Did you, Margaret? I didn't notice.'

I knew he had, but was being kind.

He added, 'Remember this, Margaret, the celebrant is always right.'

I was grateful for his support, and for the rest of the congregation that morning, from many parts of the world, who had attended the service, and by their acceptance had given me confidence. That confidence was also built as I spent the first few weeks after ordination caring for the parishes of Carlton and Drax, which included our own village of Camblesforth. Their vicar, John, was to be away on sabbatical study leave and I was asked to take the Communion services, to be there during that time, 'on loan' to them. It was just another instance of what I believe is God's wonderful sense of timing, giving me a chance to work out how best to establish my practice when being the celebrant, with the experience of slightly different traditions. I couldn't help but think back to the first time I had 'helped out' in those parishes, nearly twenty-three years previously. Their vicar was ill at that time, there was no one to help, and God had recalled me to the ministry through that situation. Now here I was as a priest in those same parishes – 'helping out' and praising the Lord for all the opportunities he had given me.

When, all those years ago, I had been praying for them, God had got me by the scruff of the neck and put me there. 'Send someone,' I had prayed, and his answer was to send me! At the same time he gave me all I needed. Looking back over the years, I realise just what a wealth of experiences he has blessed me with, of people, situations, adventures, opportunities. Yet he has never allowed me to become complacent or settled. Just when I thought I had got life organised to my own personal plan, comfortable and safe, he would disturb me, make me 'drive by the seat of my pants' and realise I could not do it alone, my strength was not sufficient; he would force me to face up to my failings and bring myself afresh to him for forgiveness, renewal and repair.

In my Bible I carry a note written to me several years ago by a small boy. I had been preaching about knowing Jesus, and following him. He, getting restless, had started writing a letter on a scrap of paper during the service. After the service his mum had come with him and said, 'Give Mrs Cundiff the letter you have written to her.'

The small boy shyly handed me his note. It read, 'Who is Jesus? I want to see him, and I can't see him. When can I see him? I wish I could. Stuart.'

I went home and wrote an answer, and when he came to church the next Sunday and came up for a blessing at the Communion rail, I handed it to him as I prayed for him. I know that letter is very special to him, as his is to me. Today I see that boy growing up into a fine young man, and I pray that he may see Jesus, and follow him all his life. His letter serves as a permanent reminder to me of what my life should be about, enabling others to see Jesus, in their homes, at school or work, in every and any situation – the Jesus who is 'the same, yesterday, today and for ever'.

I have a poster in my office. It says, 'Enjoy the miracles of each new day.' I do! For they are indeed 'new every morning'. What of the future? I can only re-echo the words, 'I do not know my future, but I know the one who holds it.'

One act of faith has been to buy myself a brand new bicycle, a bright purple one, and I enjoy the delights of the countryside around, meeting people on my travels, stopping to chat, to 'pass the time of day', giving myself space in my life to be at ease with the world around me.

'Are you one of those flying bishops?' joked a friend, noting the colour of my bicycle.

'No, a carefree Christian' – and on a bike on a lovely day, how could I be otherwise?

I do get accused sometimes of seeing the world through rose-coloured glasses, when in reality life is hard, violent, sick and sinful. But I am a realist. I live in the world, I am engaged in many difficult, sad and, yes, sometimes sickening situations. I have not been immune to trouble. Like any other family we have had our ups and downs, and in my ministry I have been hurt at times, have despaired, have been frustrated and angry. I too have gone through the 'nobody loves me' feeling at times, and lost my temper with God, other people and myself. Yet in spite of everything I am an optimist. As the little verse puts it, 'Two men looked through prison bars. One saw mud, the other stars.' I know all about the mud of life, but I don't wallow in it. Rather, I look to the one who made the stars, set them in place, and holds them and all creation, including me, safely and lovingly.

Recently I have been reading again my first book, *Called To Be Me*, and its Postscript written seven years later when I was ordained a deacon. I see how much has changed in my life since those days. I was then sure I would continue to wear my blue deaconess cassock – but now I am fully at ease in my black one. I also said I was not convinced I would wear a clerical collar and shirt, but now I happily wear them 'on duty', thankful that in these last few years clerical outfitters have realised that women clergy still want to be feminine, and so have produced for us elegant attractive designs and colours. Many of the men, too, seem to have become less stern and forbidding-looking, as they have discovered there are other colours besides black and grey available for them also. Maybe this is a fringe benefit of having women clergy! I have also passed the ripe old age of sixty, and enjoy the benefits as befits a 'senior citizen', especially the travel concessions, which I make full use of. Life goes on, and it is a good life, because God is at the centre, and I know as long as I keep close to him, and allow him to show me his way, then all will be well.

A friend I made in Oxford over forty years ago wrote to me when I was ordained priest saying,

In thinking about you the verse which came to mind was 'To shine more and more until the perfect day'. This recognition of your ministry has come to you rather late in life but if there should be a winding down of activity there need be no winding down of influence of the shining which is the result of beholding his glory, and being changed into his image. So . . . shine on!

I felt rather elderly when she spoke of 'winding down', and I certainly didn't agree that the recognition of my ministry had come rather late in life. After all, God has always recognised and encouraged me in my ministry, and where would I have been without the support of so many people? Looking back at the various stages, I would not have had it any other way. Maybe for people like myself, who have lived through the struggles and traumas of the long road to priesthood, we have been given something uniquely precious which has enabled us to 'keep on keeping on'. It has been a marvellous journey, full of interest, full of lovely people, full of encouragement and challenges.

What now? I am content to go on as God leads me, wherever he puts me. I know this, he will always be there beside me, he will never let me go, and it will never be boring, with the final destination sure and certain.

In *Called To Be Me* all those years ago, I finished by saying,

Down the road I go in my little red Polo, round the corner, through the market place, up over the bridge, and I'm on my way home. It's a great life, and I wonder, what is round the next corner?

I still feel the same, and, yes, I still drive a red Polo, although not the original one. Every day still fills me with anticipation and excitement, and I feel no signs of 'winding down' yet, as

> One more step along the world I go,
> One more step along the world I go.
> From the old things to the new,
> Keep me travelling along with you.
> And it's from the old I travel to the new.
> Keep me travelling along with you.

Amen I say to that. Amen!